Parables | *for parents*
and
other original sinners

Parables

for parents
and
other original sinners

Tom Mullen

WORD BOOKS, PUBLISHER
Waco, Texas

First Printing, September 1975
Second Printing, July 1976
Third Printing, April 1977

PARABLES FOR PARENTS AND OTHER ORIGINAL SINNERS
by Tom Mullen

Copyright © 1975 by Word, Incorporated
Waco, Texas 76703

ISBN 0-87680-434-2

Library of Congress catalog card number: 75–19896
Printed in the United States of America

to Carl and Olive

contents

preface

Robert Louis Stevenson said, "The world is full of a number of things." Parents would expand that statement somewhat because, for them, most of the things the world is full of belong to their children, and they have working parts that fall off and get stepped on in the middle of the night when you're on the way to the bathroom to fight gastritis.

About such events, this book is written, for in the experiences of being parents, unthinkable thoughts may surface: "Were I not a parent, I would have no children. Had I no children, my life would be simpler." Most of us, however, feel guilty when we have such negative thoughts, for the American Dream pictures happy families continually expressing positive feelings and exuding joy.

We know better. Life together is a picnic, but picnics include ants, warm lemonade, and the sight of the last available table being claimed by someone else. The intent of this little book is to reflect on such realities, and it starts from the premise that parents and children are able to enjoy each other more if they expect less perfection and accept the picnic for what it is, ants and all.

Thus, this is not a scientific book. It is based on the experiences and observations of one man and his family, and therefore it is loaded with subjective bias, major and minor exaggerations, and considerable nonsense. Writing the book has enabled the author to avoid committing certain crimes, particularly child abuse, and it has helped him discover why he loves and enjoys his family so much even when things get messed up. It is hoped that reading it will do the same for others. It is written from a Christian point of view and includes little "prayers" at the end of each chapter to remind us of the book's perspective.

Many thanks are due several persons, although the reader should not blame any of them for deficiencies this book contains. Most authors, as a matter of courtesy, thank their wives in the preface of their books, but Nancy Mullen deserves first mention, not because she's helped with the writing because she hasn't, but for another more significant reason. Her main contribution has been in who she is, not what she's done, which is like saying regular breathing is an important ingredient in health.

Our children—Sarah, Martha, Bret, and Ruth—obviously merit words of appreciation since their antics and attitudes inspired many of the issues herein discussed. Readers should know that the two older girls have read the manuscript and given permission for it to go to the publisher, even though their friends have promised to read the accounts of their foibles aloud in public. They are loved just as they are, and the fact they'll be different tomorrow promises a fresh opportunity to love them some more for new reasons.

Specific thanks are owed Victor Jose whose experience in riding bicycles as described in the Richmond, Indiana, *Graphic* was so similar to mine, I plagiarized some of his thoughts. Similarly, my former teacher, William Muehl, inspired the parable entitled "On Bumper Stickers and Road Signs" in an article written for *Reflection,* the alumni magazine of Yale Divinity School. Some of the chapters appeared in slightly different form in the magazine, *The Disciple,* and thanks are due its editor, James Merrell, for permission to include them here. Our faithful Earlham School of Religion secretary, Dot Toney, typed the manuscript and also did some editing, thereby sparing the reader considerable pain and the author even more embarrassment than he deserves.

Many others have said or written words that informed this book, and those anonymous sources have my gratitude. However, only the ones mentioned above could possibly have made a case in court had I failed to give them credit.

Finally, I am grateful to Carl and Olive Kortepeter, my parents-in-law, who have done many, many kind things for us over the years. Two deserve special mention. They bought over fifteen copies of my last book and gave them to relatives, a sacrificial act. Much earlier they conceived and nurtured Nancy, a tribute to their and God's creative powers. With hopes for many years of purchasing power still ahead and with love, this book is dedicated to them.

TOM MULLEN

1

On the cost of raising children

Large families were once an economic asset. When most Americans lived on farms or in small towns, boys and girls provided a source of cheap labor. Many middle-aged parents still delight in recounting the times they were up before dawn to milk cows, slop pigs, and gather eggs. Seemingly, they thought nothing of the hardship of walking four miles to school through eight inches of snow. (Editorial note: for each five years over age forty-five, add one-half mile of distance and two inches of snow).

Today, their children and grandchildren don't think much of the idea, either; and for good and bad reasons, children are no longer a financial asset. Indeed, the guy who allowed parents seven hundred fifty dollars tax exemption per child was either raised by werewolves or his kids' teeth came in straight. Parents do not bring up children these days; they finance them. A recent federal study, in fact, estimates that it costs the average family of four forty thousand dollars to raise a child from birth through college, not counting the expense of replacing lost mittens while walking to school. Nor does that figure include peanut butter and jelly, both that which is eaten and that

13

which is fed to the dog to see if it will cause its teeth to stick together.

That particular study indicated that the average cost of a first baby was $1534 with $25 added for five-foot stuffed Panda bears, exercisers, and perception-stimulators to hang from the crib, all of which are purchased by novice fathers who have not yet been billed by the hospital. Novice parents also buy books on how to raise children which are useful for keeping the crib level when a wheel falls off.

Additional children cost less, of course, primarily due to recycling of equipment, clothing, and books for keeping the crib level. (Editorial note no. 2: For each additional child, subtract 15 percent of expenses for clothing and one foot off the length of the Panda bear. After four children, statistics are not easily acquired as parents refuse to fill out forms and telephones are seldom available for personal interviews.)

Where does it all go? Contrary to the majority opinion of parents, most of the money spent on raising children does not go for soft drinks and fudge bars. Less than ten thousand dollars per year is spent on such items, and much of that amount can be subtracted from taxes as a charitable deduction since it goes to feed friends of your children who, on the basis of available evidence, are never fed at home.

Children ought not to be blamed for all the costs, however, as parents often insist upon expenses young people would happily do without, such as well-balanced meals, haircuts, and violin lessons. Nor would they be so expensive were we less eager for them to have the cultural

14

advantages we were denied, such as sets of encyclopedias and trips to museums. Many youth, in fact, long to be so denied themselves.

Parents who have four children usually support at least the same number of doctors. Obstetricians give way to pediatricians, who are supplanted by "family doctors" who share our medical dollars with dentists, orthodontists, and dermatologists. A healthy child is worth its weight in gold fillings, of course, but preventive medicine is almost as expensive as having diseases. Medical costs will vary tremendously, depending on the number of bad teeth, ruptured appendices, allergies, broken limbs, and pimples your children experience. These costs will vary also in relation to the doctor's rent district and the number of times he refurbishes his office.

It is probably *not* wise for parents to examine *all* the statistics on child-rearing, and parents of college-age young people should definitely read no further. Parents who are presently sending their children to small, private, church-related liberal arts schools will not have to worry about reading further since they can no longer afford books. It is psychologically dangerous for parents to contemplate such costs as automobile insurance rates, piano lessons (especially if you have to buy a piano), and eating in restaurants on family vacations. Not thinking about the costs of raising children may be the best option, for the only clear alternatives open to parents are bankruptcy and grand larceny.

Are they worth it? Let's face it: To a considerable number of people, children are *not* worth the expense. One needs only to hear many young couples talk about

15

being unable to "afford children" to get this message. However, it is probably the wrong question. This writer, like others with four children, will undoubtedly never get a financial return on the investment he and his wife have made. Time, money, and energy in great quantities have been invested in those children, and they seldom even clean their rooms without nagging. Indeed, as their goals and values begin to take shape, it becomes more and more obvious that they're more interested in writing poetry, provoking laughter, and saving the world than they are in making money or marrying somebody with lots of it.

Even if they showed some signs of one day paying for their existence, it is still the wrong question. The value of children we love cannot be determined by cost-accounting. It's like asking, How pretty is a flower? How many dollars' worth do you love your children? The lover who asked, "How do I love thee? Let me count the ways," had to write a poem, not submit an expense account, to answer the question.

Thus, dear reader, ignore the question, ignore statistics quoted above, and ignore the complaints that responsible parents trying to be Christian utter from time to time. We do well if we try to help our children grow and mature as people. We do better if we rejoice in who they are as they are. And we do best of all if we thank God for his gift to us of the children we have, crooked teeth and all.

Thanks, Lord, for our children, in spite of the inconveniences they cause. Help us not to confuse the cost of raising our children with their pricelessness. In the name of him who said children had a special place in the kingdom. AMEN.

2

On watching your child compete

Americans are often criticized for being a nation of spectators rather than participants. Given the enormous sums of money and amounts of time consumed in going to, attending, coming from, and offering opinions on professional sports—live or on television—such judgments may very well be accurate.

The exception, however, occurs when a parent enrolls a young child in a competitive sport. When a small boy signs up to play peewee baseball or Gra-Y football, spectatorship and participation blend in a unique way. When one's daughter is named captain of her softball team, the opportunity for *mild* involvement disappears faster than a ten-run lead in a Little League game.

Watch most organized games in which young children are competing, and you will witness extraordinary performances and many strange antics, some of which occur on the playing field. Fathers, vicariously reliving their varsity days, lunge for a first down from their seats in the stands, an action that does little to win a game but frequently bruises the ribs of those nearby. Indeed, while statistics on such matters are incomplete, more parent-

18

spectators have probably been injured watching Gra-Y football than have small boys playing the game.

Parents pace the sidelines, leap for rebounds, run the bases (in their minds), and yell a lot. In a word, they get emotionally involved. In lots of words, their verbal exhortations usually match their physical contortions, and they often exaggerate. Thus, overexuberance by mothers and fathers may account for their urging a nine-year-old, who still burns a night light in his room, to "go out and kill 'em." A few parents make helpful suggestions to the referees, too, especially when controversial decisions have been made. Some comments give directions to warmer destinations and others reveal interest in the family trees of the officials.

Youngsters frequently disappoint their parents, either by the quality of their play or by their attitude toward the sport. Some young boys have even been known to regard football as a *game* and have been observed laughing and joking with their opponents as if they were friends. Naturally, such attitudes are usually corrected by the time they reach high school, but many parents—particularly fathers who inwardly have longed since childhood to be lion tamers—suffer considerably when their own flesh and blood are unable to regard winning and losing as matters of cosmic importance. When their fouls and mistakes are announced over the loudspeaker or yelled out by the referee, the children seem to delight in the public recognition while the fathers look for something valuable under their seats. Children, furthermore, seldom stay depressed after losing, and often they use more energy crowding around the refreshment stand after the game than they did during the athletic contest.

Parents who recall that Napoleon was defeated "on the playing fields of Eton" resign themselves to the possibility that if Wellington had had *their* kids in his ranks, he wouldn't have won. For better or worse, adults who stress the importance of winning usually learn gradually to adjust their standards. After a son's team has been defeated in flag football 32–0, one learns to speak of the team's "progress"—since they lost the week before 42–0. When a daughter gets the only "hit" of the softball game on a ball that the shortstop fielded with her teeth, her father rejoices in her excellent batting stance. And when, after losing twelve straight flag football games over a two-year period, your son's team wins on a forfeit, it does not seem incongruous to dance about, slapping him and his teammates on the back while exclaiming joyfully, "Way to show up, gang!"

Obviously, some youthful teams *do* win, and the parents whose egos and self-worth are thereby enhanced find themselves tested in a different way: How does one relate (without gloating) to next-door neighbors whose kids lost? (It should be noted that the author has had little experience with this aspect of the problem.) The winners feign graciousness and say such helpful things as: "Your boy has a fine attitude." (Translation: "The kid's a loser, but he yells a lot.") Or, "He's a chip off the old block," which really means "Breeding will tell."

Losing parents show their teeth in what they hope is a smile although a beet-red face and quivering lips may more accurately indicate their honest feelings. Comments such as "You've got a tough little rascal there" allow social amenities to be observed without expressing one's real evaluation: "Your kid's the greatest menace since Jack the Ripper!"

All of which goes to show that one's ability to practice the virtues of patience, forbearance, and justice is sorely tested when one is emotionally involved. Indeed, our Christianity may most vividly be on display in the unguarded moments of life—those split-second occasions when referees, children, neighbors, and fate conspire to try our very souls.

What's a parent to do? To live a guarded life is not a solution, for to remain aloof from involvement—real or vicarious—is to miss out on joy as well as pain, satisfaction as well as disappointment. Keeping perspective about what is ultimate and penultimate, important and unimportant, will help. So will cold showers and a few laps around the block. And if all else fails, we may have to hunt up an eye witness to our childhood performances and hear a recounting of our own childhood feats. Those memories may very well provide the sobering influence we need for the living of these days and the watching of our children's games.

O God of both winners and losers, help us to see clearly and react fairly when our children compete in a little Big game. Enable young and old to be good sports. And if it be your will, grant some of us more opportunities to practice being good winners. In the name of him who kept his priorities in order. AMEN.

21

3

On children in church

The sight of an entire family in church on a Sunday morning is inspiring. One gets a warm feeling around the heart at the picture of two parents and four freshly scrubbed and neatly dressed children sitting in a row, for, verily, togetherness is what churchgoing is intended to be.

That heart-warming scene, of course, is seldom constant for an entire hour of worship. Indeed, whatever family portraits are produced after arrival, many American Christians will testify that getting there is *not* half the fun. Helping small children get dressed, for example, is seldom an edifying experience, and on Sunday mornings when all members of the family, including the dog, want to use the bathroom at the same time, one can make a persuasive argument for celibacy.

Wearing one brown sock and one red sock to church is probably not of ultimate importance, but doing so seems to have a negative effect on parents who are tempted to do violence to a small child immediately before going to learn of the love and mercy of God. Nor do fathers (who manage to get dressed, eat breakfast, and read the Sunday paper all by themselves) ease tensions by honking the horn as they wait impatiently in the car.

Furthermore, togetherness in church is sometimes a good reason for separateness. A small child has been known to inquire, immediately after the first hymn, "How much longer do we have to sit here?" Indeed, the timing of adolescent remarks during the worship of Almighty God is remarkable. Blurting out "I'm hungry" as the communion trays are passed is definitely not part of any known liturgical order, and the Apostles' Creed is scarcely improved by the whispered comment "I need to go to the baf'room" at the very moment the rest of the congregation is descending into hell.

Some parents respond to such comments by gripping a child's leg in a conscious effort to restore order and a subconscious attempt to cause excruciating pain, all the while appearing to be deeply engrossed in the sermon. Other small children in the family, delighted to see their siblings suffering, will frequently employ attention-getting mechanisms of their own. One particular mechanism that unfailingly gets attention is the contortion of sliding down in the pew until the child's neck is parallel to the seat while she attempts to remove a hymnal from the rack with her feet.

Whether successful or not, the effort produces considerable bumping and kicking of the pew in front on which several people are sitting who, it is safe to say, did not come to church to be kicked in the back. No verbal recriminations are ever uttered, of course, but recipients have been known to turn slightly during the closing hymn and smile kindly, as if to say, "*My* children never behaved like *that!*"

Frequently congregations have been treated to the sound of falling objects as little persons play in mommy's purse or contribute their coins to the offering plate. Coins and marbles (how *do marbles* get to church?!?!) usually roll a long way, often traveling down the slanted floor, across the aisle, and into a heating duct. Entire congregations have been known to pause in such moments in hushed expectancy not unlike a mystical experience—yet, not much like one either.

What, fellow churchgoers, is a parent to do? Nurseries, children's sermons, and junior church are all efforts to make church "relevant" to the family unit. All are only partially successful as wiggling and worship are synonymous with children and church.

Perhaps the presence of children is a test of the quality of the fellowship. If parents can know their fellow members understand (and forgive), they in turn will convey less anxiety to their children. If children know and love the people they see each Sunday morning, perhaps it will be less an occasion to be endured and more one to be enjoyed. If churches take the presence of children seriously and speak in language and liturgy that they understand, they might be amazed at what is grasped and appreciated.

What we know for sure is that Jesus encouraged his disciples to let the children come to him without hindrance. So be it. Let's keep bringing children to church.

Nonetheless, many parents will prefer the King James translation of that verse, for it says, *"Suffer* the little children to come."* With that, they can identify!

O God, help us to behave like Christians in church. Grant to parents the common sense to remove truly disruptive children, and give us all the gift of concentration that will overcome distractions. In the name of him who went off by himself when he really wanted to pray. AMEN.

4

On slumber parties

Anthropologists have expended considerable energy and time in examining isolated communities of South Sea Islanders or newly discovered African cultures. The information they have collected has added greatly to the literature about tribes and intentional communities, but this is *not* the kind of help most parents of teenage children need. Of much more importánce is some understanding of certain forms of American "tribalism"—particularly that adolescent phenomenon known as the "slumber party."

The phrase *slumber party* may be the most misnamed of all misnomers. As ungrammatical as it sounds, mostly what teenagers do at slumber parties is *not* sleep. Indeed, there is an unspoken commitment on the part of participants to keep one another awake. Such a commitment, it can fairly be added, is the *only* thing left unspoken, as talking ceases only when a parent wanders through the room on his fourteenth unsuccessful attempt to gain entry to the bathroom.

The relationship between parents and their children is sorely tested by a slumber party, as one's firstborn who

26

may freely share all her crises with mom under normal circumstances becomes suddenly aloof in the presence of her favorite friends. Conversation with adults is limited to bare essentials, such as: "Is there any more chip dip?" or "Gosh, mom, does dad *have* to use the phone tonight?" Other than these mountaintop exchanges, all adults are treated with perfunctory politeness, an attitude like that observed in prisoners of war who reveal only their name, rank, and serial number.

Verbal exchanges among teenagers, however, are non-stop and mind-boggling in scope. One major category of subject matter might be titled "verbal cannibalism," as absent friends and enemies alike are devoured without mercy. For example:

"I don't like Jane."

"Why?"

"Because of that pony tail she wears."

"Why don't you like pony tails?"

"Because that kind of person always wears them!"

When not devouring each other, slumber partygoers are devouring enough food to produce gastritis for an entire nation. Parents, who weighed the formulas of their infant children with scientific precision, experience culture shock as they witness young girls in dainty nighties consume quantities of pizza and Coke that have to be paid for to be believed!

Background music for this eating orgy is provided by a huge stack of records producing many decibels of noise. They also produce swinging and swaying in their listeners, a remarkable feat when one considers that many of them are simultaneously balancing hot pizza and cold soda, while talking nonstop on a phone to a dear friend they had not heard from for at least fifteen minutes. Others, of course, concentrate intensely on the music, which causes a faraway look in their eyes comparable to the Hindu experience of Nirvana or the American phenomenon of indigestion.

As the night wears on and parents wear out, the girls put up their hair. It is a commentary on our civilization that basically attractive young females can, after hours of dipping and pinning, rolling and teasing, wetting and drying, combing and brushing, produce an appearance that looks very much like an aborigine with a television antenna in her hair. Such self-torture is endured, of course, so that the girls can look beautiful for three hours the next day—if their heads don't explode overnight.

Slumber parties, in short, produce total exhaustion, upset stomachs, and migraine headaches. They also have negative physical effects on the girls! Even so, teenage girls will talk for days about how late they stayed awake, the stories they shared, and the great time they had. Parents, on the other hand, seldom mention parties they have chaperoned, as it is characteristic of most humans to repress painful experiences.

Such repression might not occur, however, if adults could see the slumber party for what it is—a ritual of growing up. The group is important to an adolescent, and parental toleration of it is a way—albeit painful—of saying, "I love you *and* your friends." It is sometimes not

28

enough to love just one's own children, as their peers are often extensions of themselves.

Christian parents want their deeds to express their feelings of affection, and they will endure considerable suffering to do so. Whether a slumber party is an appropriate expression is not clear, as no living adult has been able to stay awake the entire time. Nevertheless, Christian parents say they will risk their lives for their children, and faith without works is dead—as dead as one feels the morning after such a long, long night.

O God, who protects the stomachs and eardrums of young girls, give their mothers and fathers patience that passeth understanding. Guard the house against party-crashers, and let love grow between parents and children. In the name of him who suffered little children. AMEN.

5

On summer vacations

A summer is divided into three parts: anticipation, vacation, and recuperation. The first part may be the best part, for if it weren't for the fun of anticipating the pleasures of travel and the thought of telling about a trip when you got back, nobody would ever go very far from home.

Studies show, in fact, that more people seek help from psychiatrists *after* vacations than any other time. Vacations, it seems, often turn out to be traumatic experiences, hence recuperation is often necessary. Nevertheless, most of us need breaks from our regular routines, and getting away from it all is one way to escape the common adventures of life. So, each year, thousands of Americans leave home to have fun no matter how much suffering this entails.

One popular form of vacation that is definitely a break from the regular routine is a camping trip. Indeed, when a politician reports that one-third of the nation is now ill-fed, ill-housed, and improperly clothed, this is a sure sign that camping season has arrived. Small children and family dogs love to go camping, and they usually suffer no ill effects, probably preferring dirt with their meals. Nor do they seem bothered by the inconvenience of building fires or carrying water, especially since they are usually off chasing butterflies at such times. Parents, especially mothers, find such a life-style less a *break* from their daily routines and more of a compound *fracture.* As one mother described her camping experiences: "I haven't had so much fun since the last time I cleaned the oven."

Reactions such as these have led to more complicated forms of camping, and many families—after loading their trailers and packing their cars—could rent their houses unfurnished. Indeed, in the summer it is easy to spot the man who has everything, for when he's on vacation it's strapped to the top of his car. It is a sign of our times that in one Iowa park, so many coffee pots, television sets, electric guitars, razors, and portable refrigerators were plugged in at one time, the transformer exploded.

Given the pressure to find sufficient camping space in the wilderness, many families resign themselves to less complicated arrangements and make do as best they can in air-conditioned motels with real beds and house-broken mosquitoes. More parents than is now the case would choose to stay in motels on vacation were it not for large costs and small children. Even in those places which provide "free" accommodations for children (for a small extra fee), staying in a motel in this century is seldom an inexpensive proposition. Food costs come in two categories—high and out of sight. The daily special at the friendly, family restaurant seems to have the Rockefellers as the "family" it had in mind, and the menu features exotic food at ridiculous prices. For example, "All the lobster you can eat for $49.95."

Travelers compensate for such exploitation either by eating less food or finding a budget (translation: very cheap) eating place. Thus, to the delight of the children, a daily menu on vacation may consist of soft ice cream and hard submarine sandwiches, so called because they keep surfacing . . . surfacing . . . surfacing. Green leafy vegetables are eaten only as punishment for getting sick on the back seat of the car, and the vacation version of a well-balanced meal is a hamburger *with* tomato and lettuce.

Even when a family is willing to invest its life savings and travel in style, making the trip with children means getting there is not half the fun. The late Robert Bench-ley once said that there are only two ways to travel: first class or with children. Young children at a motel run everywhere at the top of their lungs. Ten-year-olds complain all year that there's nothing new, then sit reading comic books as you drive through Yellowstone. Children visit souvenir shops and buy tin placards that say, "Have a Good Day," which later clutter up their dressers and cause their mother to have a bad day when she dusts.

Fortunately, most vacations end in the nickel of time, to coin a phrase. A well-planned trip will allow a few days at the end for rest and relaxation, and parents will be armed with excellent excuses for not doing anything that is supposed to be fun. The really fortunate families may even have enough time left over to sleep late, bumble their way through chores, and accomplish nothing that is meaningful. Moral obligations for family togetherness having been fulfilled, families can relax and enjoy each other's company.

Please understand. Vacations provide an important aspect of our education that must not be neglected. If we get away from our daily routines, we will be able to appreciate them for the orderly, stabilizing forces they are. Our homes, crab grass and all, never look so good as after long trips in small cars with short-tempered children.

Even more important is the fact that vacations can teach us patience. If in the confines of tight space and under the pressure of high prices, we can love and forgive one another, vacations will be worth taking as well as coming home from. Patience is the ability to care slowly. It is the ability to postpone anger for a while longer. In family life there is a need for vacations from routine, but never from patience with one another. That single virtue can enable parents and children to survive hard times— famine, flood, explosions, and vacations—with equanimity and maybe even joy.

O God, who stuck with the Israelites as they grumbled in the wilderness, be with us at home and away. Grant us a little more patience, especially when we carry the extra burden of enjoying ourselves. In the name of him who was tempted in the wilderness. AMEN.

6

On hanging out in shopping centers

A phenomenon of our decade is the growth and popularity of the shopping center in suburbs and cities across the land. Next to time spent on the job and at home, countless Americans are spending the largest part of their time at the malls. In fact, the shopping center has, in many communities, replaced the old corner drug store, the city park, and Main Street as a place to go and "hang out."

Going to the mall is really a new form of the old practice of "going to town on Saturday night," the main difference being that people often go three or four times a week. Visit almost any large shopping center, and a cross section of America's passing parade will be on display. Elderly people sit on benches and gossip, talking mainly about the odd-looking teenagers who spend hours walking back and forth to see who else is walking back and forth. Little children are present in large numbers, enticed there by the promise of a sixty-second ride on an automatic pony that usually is out of order, a fact discovered by a parent two seconds after depositing a quarter.

Indeed, a veritable garden of delights awaits visitors

to many of the huge malls in or near large cities. It is commonplace to find enclosed, air-conditioned shopping malls with one hundred thirty stores, ten sets of escalators on three levels, nine thousand parking spaces, and two public restrooms. The latter conveniences are always located in the same places in every mall in America, namely, the geographically farthest possible point from where you are standing when a seven-year-old whispers the mathematical message: "Daddy, I have to do No. 1 right now!"

When one is not in a restroom or looking for one, however, there is no lack of amusements, activities, and special events. In some malls it is possible to attend an animal show, go to church, ice skate, or take karate lessons. Malls often sponsor fashion shows, art displays, frog-jumping contests, and other cultural events. Some people even enter the stores and purchase things.

For many families today's shopping malls represent a classic example of the tail wagging the dog. The fringe benefits and services of a center have come to be more important to the public than the purchase of goods and materials. Merchants respond to this need by hiring clowns, dancing girls, and high-school dropouts dressed as monkeys to bring in customers. Most of these promotional efforts are successful, and many stores are soon filled with hundreds of children being yelled at by their parents.

Occasionally young boys will organize a soccer game at one end of the mall, using the open expanse of terrazzo floor for a playing field and the double-door entrance to Sears as a goal. Teenage girls amuse themselves in other

35

ways, the most popular one being the game called "try on clothes." While statistics are not universally kept in this department, at least two young people close to the author once tried on fourteen sweaters, eleven blouses, seven pairs of slacks, and one dress (to please their mother) within an hour. All of the items, it can be reported, were "darling."

Parents, who came to buy one bottle of Pepto-Bismol and leave, pass the time in less interesting ways. Mostly they wait for Cinema I, II, or III to regurgitate its horde of patrons, among whom is one of their children whose life would have been ruined without seeing *Airport '75* (or *'76, etc.*). While waiting, the smaller children play "getting lost," a game so popular that some shopping malls have employees just to locate run-away or lost children.

Elaborate procedures are established to find children who have disappeared, once parents rise above the deeply felt temptation not to look for them. The mother walks through the toy departments on the upper level of the south side of the mall, planning to join her husband at the ice cream store under the big chocolate cone when she has made her rounds. The father's route takes him in the opposite direction, in and out of the penny arcade where everything costs a nickel, past the hot-pretzel vendor, through the motorcycle display, and back to chocolate. Should either parent discover the missing child en route, he or she is to go immediately to the nearest music shop and play "Stars and Stripes Forever" on an organ with all stops pulled out.

Somehow families manage to be reunited, and another evening of separated togetherness is climaxed by its attendant feelings of complete exhaustion. Certain psychological needs are probably met, though, as the shopping center phenomenon has been analyzed by experts who conclude that hanging out and milling about such malls enable feelings of loneliness somehow to be dissipated. Young people are near other young people, children get parental attention, and parents grow closer together as they face each successive crisis.

Going as a family provides a special benefit that might not otherwise be experienced. Caring, sharing, worrying families discover they have each other in the midst of a crowd, and they are spared the sense of isolation that others, wandering aimlessly, may feel. For those so blessed with a place in a family unit, a special insight into modern life can be learned: Shopping centers are fun to visit but it's great not to have to live there.

Father of us all, watch over all the lonely people wherever they go to escape their loneliness. Be with those families wandering the malls; may they get together when their day is done. In the name of him for whom his parents had to go looking, too. AMEN.

7

On summer camp

By July 3 approximately four million American children
are in summer camp. This is one of the reasons why so
many parents celebrate the Fourth of July.

Do not misunderstand. American parents love their
children most of the time, and they are happy to have
them around the house some of the time. Nevertheless,
absence helps the head stay saner, to coin a phrase, and
many married adults have been known to do little jigs in
the street right after the bus for camp moves out of sight.

To passers-by such behavior is regarded as strange,
possibly even deviant, but to veteran camper-parents who
have overcome guilt feelings about enjoying time without
their children, it is totally natural and appropriate. Parents who are sending an eight- or nine-year-old off for the
first time, of course, may respond differently, such as by
crying or hugging their children vigorously while gushing
such endearments as "Goodbye, baby" or "Don't forget
to brush your teeth!" These responses are treated with
complete contempt by veteran parents, but they so totally
humiliate the child that parting quickly becomes a bless-
ing rather than a sorrow.

Summer camps, whether they be church, YMCA, 4-H,

Scout, or sports camps, are almost always staffed by unmarried college students. Having decided that they someday want "to work with children," they commit themselves to camp responsibilities and leadership tasks with enthusiasm and dedication. They "understand" young boys and girls, and some of them even sleep in the very same cabins and tents with the campers.

Such dedication may explain why the American population in recent years has been near zero growth, for short-sheeted beds, sand in sleeping bags, and frequent midnight pillow fights contribute mightily to disenchantment with the institution of marriage and parenthood. Student counselors learn quickly the value of discipline and orderliness, as well as the importance of treating each camper as an individual. The latter is accomplished by establishing close personal relationships with one's charges and, when in doubt, peeking at the name tags in the kid's underwear. Such shortcuts can be hazardous, however, for if a mother forgets to sew name tags to her son's T-shirts, he may be called "Fruit of the Loom" for the rest of his life.

Children learn many important skills at summer camp. They learn how to swim, shoot bows and arrows, and bead headbands. Perhaps unintentionally, they also learn a lot about survival training, discovering that—contrary to parental preaching—one can make it through a day without brushing, without sleeping in pajamas, and without eating vegetables. Such discoveries seem to build enormous camaraderie among young boys who rejoice in the fellowship of bad breath and crusty clothing.

Meanwhile, back at the ranch-style house, parents begin to wonder how Johnny or Mary is getting along, or even if he or she is alive. Having written twice a day so that one's child would not seem forgotten at mail call, a parent may feel some anxiety when *no word* whatsoever is received in return. Veteran parents, however, have learned that some news is worse than no news, for what is left unsaid in a child's letter often boggles the mind. ("Dear Mom and Dad, I am O.K. Camp is fun and the fire didn't burn much. Love, Bret.")

Other letters may bring inexperienced parents to the very brink of a visit or even recall as homesickness pops out between the lines. ("This camp has everything. It doesn't need me. My undying love, Ruthie.") Still other correspondence demonstrates growing independence, as in "My counselor said I should write home at least twice. This is once."

Indeed, the return home from camp is often a significant moment in the relationship of children and parents. To please their parents, some perceptive children will rumple their pajamas and squeeze toothpaste out of the tube as if they had been used. Others will surprise their mothers with the pet garter snakes they captured in the woods "all by themselves," an event which often reestablishes the parent-child line of authority very quickly.

Mostly, however, what summer camp helps us learn is that we need vacations from one another. In one sense good parents conscientiously push their children out of the home. Their goal is to help dependent children become independent adults. The feelings of missing and being missed show that love continues, and the discovery

40

that parents and children can enjoy each other's absence is a step toward maturity for both. Besides, the fact that a child didn't change his underwear for a week means there is work yet to be done.

O Ruler of Nature, thank you for protecting children and camp staff among your other mighty acts. Help us as we stretch the ties that bind. In the name of him who promised us a Counselor. AMEN.

8

On amusement parks

The Puritan ethic, which gets blamed for uptightness and narrow-mindedness, has clearly been overcome in one area of American life. No longer is "having fun" suspect. In fact, the opposite is true: Having fun is almost obligatory and at moments seems to be a national compulsion. In 1975, report those who keep track of such things, Americans spent close to 250 billion in the "fun market," a sizable chunk of which was left behind in amusement parks by parents indulging their children.

Today's amusement park is a phenomenon in its own right and a far cry from the dusty, rickety, and litter-strewn permanent carnivals which added so little to the skylines of cities in America. Schools now rent buses to take children to King's Island or Knotts Berry Farm for field trips. Church groups in Florida head for Bible World where they can witness puppet shows in the David and Goliath Theater and, with the flip of a switch, view the burning bush or Jesus floating in the air.

Parents who attempt to deny their children the chance to visit an amusement park may be tried for abuse and neglect although a jury of adults will never convict them. The reality is that weekends at ye olde amusement park do not allow us to return home refreshed, as after fun, but too pooped to pop, as after an ordeal.

A day at the amusement park begins innocently enough as several thousand families arrive simultaneously and early in order to beat the crowds. Huge asphalt lots enable families to park their cars in the same county with the shuttle bus lines where, after a long walk, buses can be boarded which deposit their riders at the very gate of the park.

Families who have planned ahead are not shocked by the admission fee which is about seven dollars per person or forty-two dollars for a family of six, a sum which is equivalent to the interest payments on a second mortgage or the amount of money earned from eight weeks of delivering papers in the rain. Armed guards are on duty, vigilant and alert for little customers short enough to slip under the turnstiles, and firmly turning back any adults carrying picnic baskets.

Picnicking is discouraged at many amusement parks because management provides exotic eating places within the park for gracious dining and well-balanced meals at prices any Arab oil sheik could afford. Dining is "gracious" because that's the word people often use who don't swear when they learn that hot dogs cost eighty-five cents each and soft drinks fifty cents per four-ounce cup. Meals are "well balanced" because parents learn to be contortionists as they carry burgers, French fries, and big orange drinks to their children who are too busy watching the fat lady soaking her feet in the fountain to help.

The real attraction of an amusement park, of course, is not its food, as unforgettable as it might be. That which brings them in and back and back again are the rides. Children who get car sick ten minutes after pulling out of the driveway will spend an entire afternoon riding upside down, hanging over, falling backward, or plummeting down at a seventy-five degree angle. Even first-graders who sleep with stuffed animals for security have no fear of the roller coaster, especially when accompanied by their daddies who are terrified.

When daddies accompany their children on the roller coaster, however, their fear of dying is quickly replaced by the absolute, unavoidable certainty of vomiting. Even when vomiting itself is not experienced, a feeling remains in the pit of the stomach not unlike acute appendicitis.

There is usually plenty of time to recover from one ride before going on another since long lines of willing victims wait a half-hour or more to experience a three-minute ride in a hollowed-out log boat or a drive-it-yourself jalopy. Many of the approaches to the rides, in fact, feature a maze of metal alleys which guide riders to their dates with destiny. These are not unlike cattle chutes into which animals are funneled shortly before they are slaughtered, an analogy which is apt in several ways.

Most of these sons of Disneyland advertise that they provide a "Spanking-clean entertainment package for the entire family." Such claims, based on this observer's experience, are true. The entertainment is clean and a lot of spanking goes on inside the park. As they wait in line, the signs of boredom and fatigue on the faces of adults and children tell a tale of irony. Tempers flare, arguments rage, and frustration abounds. The promise of fun either never materializes or departs so suddenly that even a first-grader knows she's been ripped off.

Parents, who begin to worry in the middle of the afternoon whether they'll be able to afford both an orange drink *and* the next car payment, are cheered very little by the "oompa" band as it plays the "Beer Barrel Polka" for the fourteenth time. Some adults may even come to understand in a fresh way the truth of H. L. Mencken's statement: "No one ever went broke by underestimating the taste of the American public."

Still we go. And we go again. Some seem to have fun, and a few testify afterwards that a good time was had by all. The ones who manage a good time, however, are probably the same persons who enjoy each other and what life brings them wherever they are. They know that to miss going to Coney Island, Disneyland, Six Flags over Mid-America, or The Land of Oz will not ruin their lives. The truth is that those people who are able to have good times have discovered an axiom of ancient wisdom: "We find only the fun we bring with us." The fun we bring with us is one item that never has to be checked at the gate.

O God, watch over us when we ride the roller coaster with our children. Spare us the need to accompany them on the Zinger. Fill us with an enthusiasm for life that will free us to enjoy each day with or without amusement parks. In the name of him who showed us the abundant life. AMEN.

9

On riding bicycles

American adults need only a crisis to find new ways to cause themselves pain. Thus, in the name of the energy crisis, or the air pollution crisis, or the tight-money crisis (choose one), thousands of otherwise rational persons have purchased bicycles for transportation. Some claim to ride merely for exercise, and an occasional fanatic will suggest that a long, relaxed ride down a hill on a bike brings him closer to nature. He does not, of course, indicate what the laborious ride up that hill he coasted down brings him closer to, other than exhaustion.

Whatever the reason, there is no doubt that bicycling is one of the most rapidly growing forms of recreation in America. Tired of commercial pressures from automobile makers, bicyclers have caused a whole new industry to bloom which is applying its own pressure. Bike stores are popping up in large cities and small towns, selling not only bicycles but also tents, sleeping bags, pans, stoves, and first-aid kits that attach to bikes.

That last item—the first-aid kit—is a significant one. Bicycling can be a relaxing and leisurely sport, but the nation has not yet geared down for bikes. Traveling across city streets on a bicycle is comparable in courage only to Lindbergh's flight across the Atlantic, albeit less safe. No sound is more terrifying to a cyclist than the roar of a semi-trailer passing on his left while leaving approximately eighteen inches of space between twelve thousand pounds of truck and the curb for one frail bicycle and a very nervous rider.

Indeed, drivers of cars, and especially trucks, seem to resent the presence of bicycles on "their" streets. How else can we explain the fact that engines are revved up as they pass: buzz—rumble—zarah—room! And how explain the vision of a grinning truck driver looking down on a helpless rider other than to surmise his smile is either evidence of sadistic impulses or brain damage suffered as a child from chewing the paint off his tricycle.

Clearing major intersections are also unraveling experiences for the rider. To be fair, all the danger in this adventure is not the fault of the automobile drivers who merely resent the rider because he, on his two-wheeler, can make better time in the rush-hour traffic than they can. One can even forgive the occasional driver who honks his horn and squeals his brakes at the very moment you sought to turn left, a reaction that is a sure cure for low blood pressure.

No, much of the danger of bike riding is generated by the nature of the machine itself. Modern bicycles, for example, have seats, but they evidently are not for sitting. In fact, they seem designed for making one sorry he does, and they are set on many bikes at an altitude six inches higher than was once thought possible to raise that part of the anatomy while reaching down to grasp the handlebars which, to any adult observer, seem to have been attached upside down. Riding in this position is supposed to give maximum thrust to one's leg power, but as one rides about with his posterior elevated, his arms extended, his neck bent backwards, and his eyes squinted from tears and perspiration, the tendency is to run into parked cars.

Ten-speed gears on bicycles are supposed to alleviate much of the pain, of course. On hills they allow you to move from a high-ratio gear, where you painfully pedal very slowly and get there very quickly, to a low-ratio gear where you pedal like mad and get practically nowhere. Middle-aged bikers soon learn that all gears are the same —low—and those who continue to ride for all those good reasons mentioned above usually confine their routes to those portions of bike paths appropriate to their age and condition: abandoned runways on perfectly level ground far from sadistic truck drivers and scoffing neighbors.

Whatever else it does, the return to bicycling tells us an important truth about ourselves and our civilization. We try to return to basics, to simple ways of doing things, when the world becomes burdensomely complicated. When we do, we discover two things: The world remains complicated and threatening to our efforts to be simple, and so we complicate our simplicities with more gears, better tires, fancier brakes, and dandier handlebars. Our ultimate goal, at least subconsciously, is to build a bike big enough and powerful enough to scare a truck!

Better that we rejoice in the world as God made it,

accepting our man-made complications for what they are, and live as simply as we can in the face of the terrors of the day and the aching muscles of the night.

O God, thank you for the inventive powers of persons. Help us to use them to keep your creation as free as possible from pollution, noise, and traffic. Watch over all bicycle riders, young and old, especially at the rush hour. In the name of him who had the good sense to walk across Galilee. AMEN.

10

On gardens and their victims

Nostalgia about "the land" is abroad in the land. Now that many more than half of all Americans live in cities with attendant miseries, the idyllic life of the farm seems attractive as never before. The publishers of the *Whole Earth Catalog* have responded to this longing, and they have made a pile of money extolling the simple, frugal life.

For most of us, however, the range of opportunities for return to simple living is narrow. Few of us who do not now live on farms are going to move to them very soon, and the dream of pork chops from our own pigs, milk from our own cows, and eggs from our own chickens will come true only to the extent we share life vicariously with the Waltons on TV.

What seems to be within our grasp, however, and therefore is attempted with an optimism that makes Norman Vincent Peale appear introverted, is the family garden. Gardens do not require large plots of land, the gardener's manual explains, to produce "abundant amounts of vegetables for an entire family." The impression is clearly left that one merely drops seeds into

51

the ground and jumps back before a stalk of corn pokes him in the eye. Would-be gardeners who think in these terms are in for a root awakening, for seed catalogs are a popular form of science fiction. There is reason to believe that the pictures they contain are posed by professional plants and flowers at fifty dollars an hour.

Not highlighted in seed catalogs, whole earth catalogs, and gardening magazines are weeds, blisters, and vegetable miscarriages. It is instructive to recall the parable of the sower in this regard and remember that three out of four of those gardens didn't make it. Scripture continues to be fulfilled, too, as thorns, birds, and rocks remain the natural enemies of all us who wish to turn up a rutabaga with our bare toe and eat it on the spot (the rutabaga, not the bare toe).

Preparing the soil requires either cheap tools and hard work, or expensive Rototillers and soft money. Some gardeners use so much fertilizer the garden ends up eating better than they do. Planting the seeds demands water, much of which is provided by Mother Nature at inopportune times and some of which is delivered through nearly as many feet of hose as there are in the Alaska pipeline. The combination of properly prepared soil, ample water, and sunshine produces plants and vines almost as sturdy as the weeds which try to choke them to death.

Cultivation of the garden—a polite phrase describing chopping big weeds with a heavy hoe and crawling on the ground extracting tiny ones with blistered fingers—builds character and allows one's corn to grow large enough for the neighborhood raccoons to eat. One's faith is deepened, too, as the Lord giveth and the aphids, chinch bugs, and cutworms taketh away.

The indignities and discouragements described above could be managed were it not for the existence of God's chosen few—the successful gardeners. Their gardens are always located nearby and are distinguished by straight rows, lush tomatoes, and immaculate cultivation. Created and maintained by 4-H graduates with green thumbs clear up to their elbows, such gardens stand as living testimonies to the verity that hard work is rewarded if you're lucky. Their success, obviously, helps others produce a bumper crop of sour grapes.

These veterans offer helpful advice. ("Your corn would have been better if it had grown more than eighteen inches.") They are understanding and sympathetic. ("I had bad luck with my garden once back in 1947.") Most humiliating of all is their generosity as they give you whole baskets of tomatoes, dozens of ears of juicy corn, and bunches of radishes, while you ate your whole garden in one meal. Providentially, the hundreds of hours spent on one's knees pulling weeds make it possible to accept the gifts graciously and resist the temptation to invite them over for a cup of homemade hemlock.

Gardening may have other lessons to teach us in addition to humility. In these times when bad new days cause us to long for good old days, we can recall that it was ever so. If we mourn the passing of humanity's direct involvement with the good earth, we might temper our grief with the thoughts of twelve- and fourteen-hour days of muscle-aching drudgery, of slopping around in ankle-deep manure, of milking cows seven days a week, and of making hay in the hot sun on the Fourth of July.

Gardens, the fruitful ones and the other ones, may be helpful reminders that we are not self-sufficient. Today the average farmer produces enough food to feed fifty people, and the middle men—who neither sow nor reap—put still dewy vegetables into supermarkets while they are fresh and smelling of the earth that nourished them.

If we think about it, gardening may help us thank God for the anonymous persons who keep us alive. Nostalgia for the land or the simple life is a healthy emotion only if it doesn't prevent us from rejoicing in the blessings that today's way of doing things provides. Indeed, because a relatively few feed us and supply us with what we need, we find new freedom—to read a book, write a poem, visit the Grand Canyon, or maybe, with lots of luck, grow a garden.

Creator God, bringer of sun and rain, we thank you for the harvest and the hard work of the harvesters. If it be your will, do well enough by our garden this year that we won't have to accept vegetables from Jim Yerkes. In the name of him who sowed good seed. AMEN.

11

On bumper stickers and road signs

The passing parade of life may be more fully revealed by bumper stickers and road signs than by all the opinion polls and surveys ever taken. Indeed, one might take the pulse of America simply by driving slowly and leisurely across the United States and noting the views and attitudes expressed on the rear ends of automobiles, posted on billboards, and hand-painted on rocks and cliffs along the way.

When life was simpler, bumper stickers and road signs were also simple. Many of us, as children, used to play games in the car, having contests to see who could spot the most inspirational biblical counsels on roadside barns, rocks, and signs (Note: The winner always sat on the right side of the car). "The wages of sin is death" was frequently observed, and "Prepare to meet thy God" was another quotation that scored points and, we might add, was remembered afterward, especially if it were located at the apex of a hairpin turn.

Entire families were bound together in those simpler times by the delightful discovery of the now-vanished

Burma Shave signs. Aloud and in rhythm the unfolding messages would be chanted by young and old alike:

"She eyed		"A beard
his beard		that's rough
and said no dice	or:	and overgrown
The wedding's off		is better than
I'll cook the rice		a chaperone
Burma Shave"		Burma Shave"

Alas! With their departure in 1963 a bit of Americana died and with it some of the corniest and best-loved jingles ever created.

Whereas bumper stickers once were merely advertising announcements ("See Rock City" or "Cypress Gardens, Florida"), now they often provide messages with many social, political, or even philosophical implications. Life is heavier and more serious, and our bumper stickers reflect similar moods. As we drive along, we subconsciously decide who are the good guys and the bad guys in the cars we see. For, while other motorists may remain forever personally anonymous, their views on many issues stare back at us for mile after mile at fifty-five miles per hour.

"America—Love It or Leave It" competes for our approval with "America—Love It and Lead It." Other cars, usually Volkswagens, remind us that "Guns Can Kill!" a message which is disputed by stickers which proclaim: "When we outlaw guns, outlaws will have guns." The transitory nature of many causes is revealed when,

56

in certain parts of the country, a faded billboard or barely readable bumper sticker can still be found which asks the world to "Impeach Earl Warren" or "Get the U.S. out of the U.N. and the U.N. out of the U.S." Newer stickers, also beginning to fade, still call for impeachment, but the names have been changed.

Seldom does "Another Family for Peace" adorn a car that also demands "Support Your Local Police." Seemingly, too, an inherent contradiction is overlooked by the ecologist who places the slogan, "Stop All Pollution," approximately fourteen inches from his exhaust pipe. Male chauvinism, not so subtly veiled in Burma Shave ads, is a direct target of the sticker which reads, "Trust God—SHE Provides!" We are urged to honk if (1) "We love Jesus," (2) "Think he's guilty" (not Jesus), or (3) "Like to streak."

The marquee of one small-town chiropractor wages a continual verbal battle with physicians in general and the American Medical Association in particular. Even church bulletin boards do more than announce the time of services and catchy sermon titles. One church board, incongruously, urged a town's basketball team on to greater victories by proclaiming, "Go Get 'Em, Devils!" Apparently, no conflict of interest was involved.

All in all the abundance of signs and bumper stickers that are "relevant" to our times bespeak a kind of naive faith in the power of moral exhortation. The fact that there are so many of them may delude us—and especially those who post them—into thinking that saying words for or against causes is equivalent to doing something about them. Problems of massive complexity are transformed into slogans. No wonder one discouraged soul decided that he would only champion a cause that was too long for a bumper sticker and too insignificant for a protest march!

We may, of course, use a bumper sticker or a billboard as an outlet for being heard. As it gets more and more difficult to influence the powers and the principalities which affect our lives, at least we can let off steam and deliver a message—albeit sloganized—by putting it on our cars or painting it on a big rock at the edge of town. This will be at least as effective as carrying out the garbage in the editorial section of the newspaper with which we disagree.

The real sadness, however, is that bumper stickers and road signs cause us to prejudge people by categorizing them without ever getting to know them. Is it possible for a "War Is Bad for Children" sticker-bearer ever to be reconciled with a "Join the NOW Army" driver as they meet beside the gasoline pumps? Probably not. What we need now is the moral equivalent of Burma Shave signs that may or may not encourage us to get rid of whiskers but just might help us get closer together once again.

O Lord, help us never to relegate our heartfelt concerns to the rear ends of our cars. Enable us to love our enemies, even those whose bumper stickers disagree with ours. In the name of him who asked why this generation needed a sign. AMEN.

12

On school days

It has often been said that school days are the happiest days of your life. Most adults will wholeheartedly agree with this, providing, of course, *all* their children are old enough to go.

Those parents, especially mothers, who are privileged to share with four children the day-by-day experiences of summertime, when the living is humid, are among this country's most passionate supporters of compulsory education. Many of them, in fact, regard the reopening of school as a major contributor to mental health, second only to modern psychiatry.

Such inner feelings of joy at the sight of one's beloved children leaving the house for school should not be interpreted as evidence of lack of love by parents. Quite the contrary, it is a manifestation of a high form of love on their part, especially when alternative courses of action are considered, such as chaining children to trees and beating them with whips.

Summer, after all, means swimming, cooking out in the backyard, going on vacations, and long twilight conversations with friends. Unfortunately, it also usually includes hauling kids to and from the swimming pool, attempting to broil hamburgers over charcoal that won't light, traveling through Kansas at 102 degrees Fahrenheit to get to a Colorado vacation, and very long twilight conversations with small children who can't sleep because "it's not dark yet."

If a family adds the following, or its counterparts, to the summer schedule, the beginning of school sounds positively exotic: 4-H work (three children, eleven projects), summer school (one daughter, disgruntled; two courses, dull), day camp (one six-year-old, five days, ten roundtrips to the bus, one case of poison ivy), summer jobs (two paper routes, one library job, three lawns to mow, four babies with whom to sit), Little League (plus practices), and a family garden (countless hours resulting in many string beans, four tomatoes, and an ear of corn).

This is not to say—let the record show—that all harassment and confusion end with the first ringing of the old school bell. Indeed, the problems are merely rearranged into more orderly packages of frustrations.

For one thing, attending free public schools can be very expensive. Sending a child to school these days is very educational, as it teaches parents how to do without a lot of things. Most parents are convinced, as a matter of fact, that the road to the schoolhouse is merely a branch of the road to the poorhouse, and those newspaper articles about how to dress children inexpensively for school were written by nuns extolling poverty as a way of life.

School "needs" are well known to various commercial enterprises, particularly clothiers and crayon-makers. Back-to-school clothes never seem to turn out to be the same as come-home-from-school clothes of the preceding June. This is partly because styles change rapidly, and it is a known fact that while little children don't care what they are wearing, so long as it is dirty, all living teenagers will suffer psychological damage if new clothes for school are not purchased. The other reason, of course, is that children have been known to grow—up, out of, and around—and last year's wardrobe may be fit for a king or queen but those royal personages would necessarily have to be shorter, thinner, or narrower than the former owners.

Mostly, however, what having all your children in school at the same time means is that you're growing older. Life is lived in chapters, and the peace and quiet of a house after breakfast on the first day of school is a milestone of significance. It is a reminder that another big slice has been cut out of the umbilical cord that has made little people so dependent upon bigger people for many years. It means that a new chapter will have its own story-line, with its own special set of trials and triumphs.

It can also be its own cause for thanksgiving—for peace and tranquillity, certainly, but also for the knowledge that children do grow up and need us less (or at least in different ways). And it can also be a time to express gratitude for schools and schoolteachers who help our children leave home and leave us. It may even be that we would never be able to survive their going without the summers that anesthetize us from painful parting.

We thank you, O God, for healthy, noisy, demanding children. Help their parents cut the cords that set both free for new occasions and new duties. In the name of him whose parents didn't always understand, either. AMEN.

13

On football

Today's big game hunter is a man who switches channels all Sunday afternoon. This does not mean that the contemporary football fan is less rugged than his dedicated predecessors of yore. He, too, is ready and willing to sacrifice personal comfort, health, and family tranquillity to watch twenty-two men inflict bodily pain on one another. True, most football watching takes place in living rooms, but even under these circumstances certain mental, physical, and spiritual disciplines must be observed for serious watching to be sustained over long periods of time.

After all, with the advent of the World Football League, which plays games on Wednesday and Thursday nights, a schedule of contests now exists guaranteed to destroy dining plans all over America. With high-school football to watch on Friday nights, college games on Saturdays, and National Football League games on Sunday afternoons and Monday nights, only Tuesdays remain sans football. Furthermore, since the season begins in early July and concludes in late January, fans will necessarily have to develop both their concentration for even more crucial third down situations and their stamina for the many extra weeks of watching. Truly, the dedicated fan is a special breed, the kind of person who has helped make this country what it is today.

The purpose of this brief essay, however, is not primarily to glorify the American football fan, as he now has his reward. With six out of seven days under his control, there is a significant precedent for his resting on the seventh. No, beloved, we here need to honor those noble souls who have shared the struggles and vicariously suffered in the pursuit of happiness that watching football represents—the wives, the ones left behind to serve refreshments while others sit and watch.

True, not all wives share their husbands' dedication to football, some regarding it as merely a game. Others have been known, in moments of anger, to indulge in sarcasm, such as calling the children together and saying, pointedly, in their father's presence, "Now, children, is there anything you would like to say to your father before the season begins?" One woman, possibly a subversive, actually introduced a bill in a state legislature which would have had any man who watched more than twelve hours of football on a weekend declared legally dead!

Such women, praise the Lord, are a minority, and others have furthered the cause of equal rights tremendously by becoming knowledgeable and committed fans themselves. Most wives, however, suffer quietly on the sidelines, explaining to creditors that Mr. Jones is "in conference" (usually the Big Ten or Missouri Valley) and instructing the rescue unit which is taking one of their children to the hospital not to use its siren so as to avoid disturbing the game.

Some wives actually attend real games. A conservative estimate in a recent college game played in a bone-cold, pouring rain was that every sixth lump huddled in the stands was a woman trying to remember what she had said in her wedding vows to deserve this. Obviously, these women deserve rewards better than they usually receive —pneumonia or frostbite.

Wives married to veteran fans (root word, *fanatic*) who accompany their husbands to games provide living evidence that their marriage is intact. They learn to reckon time by game standards, knowing that the final two minutes really will last seventeen minutes and twelve seconds. They adjust to conversations that make no sense ("It was a fly pattern with the flanker doing a curl-in in the deep zone"). They learn never to ask questions ("What goes on in the huddle?"). Most of all, they avoid making moral judgments such as, "I don't think that an eight-year-old boy should carry a sign which says 'Kill the [expletive deleted].' "

The message in all this is twofold. One clear signal is that husbands and wives who really love each other can survive many differences, even the addition of the World Football League. A more important observation is that entertainment in America—in this case, football—holds high priority in many lives and often interferes with relationships, justice, truth, and righteousness. The temptations of football are like the temptations of anything else: They complicate the task of putting first things first.

Fortunately, we have Scripture to guide us, for in Matthew 6:33 we are urged to "seek first his kingdom and his righteousness" and all the rest will be extra points—er, ah, added to it.

O God, as the Great Scorer, be kind in your decisions about our priorities. Watch over football players, fans, spouses, and Tuesday nights. In the name of him who put first things first. AMEN.

14

On going home

Cynicism is a viable option in contemporary America. While every generation has its political corruption and public scandals, most of us were not prepared for the shocking revelations of the 1970s. Not only did we learn that the winner of the All America Soap Box Derby had cheated, but it turns out that the smiling, wholesome woman on the Ivory Snow box had performed in pornographic movies. Very few things were 99 44/100 percent pure.

The antidote to cynicism is a return to one's roots. At least in one's imagination, home is the one place where you won't get ripped off. Robert Frost's famous definition, "Home is the place, where, if you go there, they have to take you in," is now reversed. Home may be the *only* place where, if we go there, we *won't* be taken in.

The longing for roots and home is characteristic of most of us, especially when we feel anxious about life-in-general. Children, for example, exhibit enormous curiosity about their own history and that of their extended family. They seem fascinated with what their daddies did as little boys and eager to learn about their mothers' childhood.

While much of their interest comes at bedtime and is part of the ritual of stalling, some of it is genuine. Parents usually delight in recounting tales from their past, especially since their selective memories often make truth stranger than fiction and a thousand times more exaggerated. Even so, with all its impurities, the plea to "tell about the time when you . . ." outranks both Dr. Seuss and Louisa May Alcott as bedtime entertainment.

Parents are tempted to cash in their memories to deliver hidden lectures on child guidance, and some of their thrice-told tales about themselves make Horatio Alger sound like a grade-school dropout. If all the wood they cut for their boyhood fireplaces in zero weather were placed end to end, there would be enough for a transcontinental wiener roast. Likewise, even the most gullible child will raise an eyebrow over such claims as "we always obeyed our parents" and "we brushed our teeth after eating even though we used baking soda and had to pump the water by hand." Children, who usually check such gargantuan memories with their grandparents, know better than this, for even John-boy once disobeyed his father on national television.

Children are willing to make allowances and forgive, however, when parents recall the time the family dog was hit by a car and nursed back to health by round-the-clock efforts. They literally interrogate a parent for details when a father describes the experience of losing two dollars to a hustler at a county fair, as a small child is among the few remaining persons in America who regards two dollars as a large sum. Memories of poor beginnings, family crises, adventures with pets—such history begs to be appropriated by children, for by so doing they learn who they are.

They long to visit the actual geographical location of their parents' beginnings, and children who have living grandparents—especially those who live on the "homeplace"—are among the most blessed of humans. Many parents have to improvise, as their homeplaces have been torn down to make room for progress. It is difficult to romanticize about a Kroger parking lot where once a house stood, and few children get excited over a section of a four-lane highway even though they're told the flashing yellow light at the intersection marks the place where daddy was born.

High-school yearbooks and old photo albums also fascinate children and embarrass adults. Kids who can watch cartoons for an hour without cracking a smile will literally roll on the floor after seeing pictures of their mothers with frizzed hair and skirts three inches above the ankle. Near-hysteria is produced by a photograph of their father wearing a crew cut. ("Daddy, you look like a prisoner of war.") Open-mouthed incredulity is expressed upon learning that it was once possible to put on your pants without taking off your shoes.

In all the nostalgia and search for roots, there is also a search for fundamental values. What is really important? Whom can we really trust? What really matters?

The answer is not a new one, for when the ancient Hebrews found themselves in trouble, they invariably looked back to their beginnings for compass points to follow. They remembered that they were the people who came out of Egypt, who had Abraham, Isaac, Jacob, and Joseph as their ancestors. The dangers in looking back are many, not the least of which is to substitute sentimentality for truth or to rejoice in the past and overlook the joys of the present. Still, if a child can know he or she has a past and it has a connection with the present, the future seems less ominous.

This interest in family history holds great promise for present-day parents, too. As their memories get fuzzier, the events of their lives can take on new potential for embellishment. Best of all, they have in their possession many pictures and yearbooks featuring their own children dressed in psychedelic shirts, bell-bottom pants, and the "layered look." These will surely send their children's children into orbit, and that is an unbeatable incentive for living a long life.

O God, our help in ages past, watch over our "homeplaces" however rundown they may be. Keep us in touch with our past, so our present will make some sense. In the name of him who was in the line of David. AMEN.

15

On showing slides, alas!

Where two or three are gathered for some reason, there in the midst of them will be an amateur photographer taking pictures. Many a wedding has been made unforgettable by Uncle George's popping up in the third row to explode flashbulbs in the faces of a bride and groom already in a state of shock. For others, no birthday or celebration would be complete without pictures for the family album, and the candid camera-person is as much a part of the family scene as hot dogs, apple pie, and stomach cramps.

Nor is it exclusively the major events of life which get recorded. Washing the dog, the loss of a child's front tooth, or neighborhood garage sales are often captured on film. How many distinguished Americans, in fact, have been and will be embarrassed by the public viewing of their bare baby bottoms taken by ecstatic parents who never before had seen anything so adorable? Indeed, in some families children become conscious of which is their best side long before they learn to keep it covered.

Amateur photographers differ from professionals in two important ways. (1) Professionals usually take better pictures. Viewing a slide-show of fuzzy pictures is a lot like forgetting to take your glasses along when you visit Europe. (2) Professionals don't talk about their equipment so much. Indeed, conversations between two shutterbugs consist of a special language, full of symbols, letters, and numbers that make understanding the Book of Revelation seem simple by comparison.

For example, consider the following conversation: "I used a Spectra Professional with direct F/Stop readings and integrated light measurements to get my kid's chicken pox, and it was like having the disease!" Response: "Yes, but if you had used my Mike/Lite bracket and CP-16 Relex camera with its RE50 microphone, you could have captured her cries of pain as well!"

Most of us really don't mind the funny ways and words of amateur photographers, especially if we get in enough pictures ourselves. However, no invitation inspires panic to quite the degree than those chilling after-dinner words: "And now we'd like to show slides of our trip to Italy last summer." (Note: Substitute "Holy Land" or "Bangkok" or "Kansas City," depending upon what your repressed memory bank allows.)

To be fair, an occasional slide show will be brief enough, with several interesting pictures, and have a sufficiently entertaining commentary to make the evening better than being at a PTA meeting. However, fairness also demands that it be publicly declared what has been privately thought by many such captured audiences for years: "O Lord, why me?"

The darkness of the room is frequently the best part

72

of the show, as it conceals yawning, sleeping, and grimaces of despair. The worst part is experienced when uninteresting pictures are accompanied by equally fascinating commentary. In fact, the old cliche, "A picture is worth a thousand words," does not apply to most slide shows. In them, we get both.

Amateur photographers usually take pictures of that which interests them the most, which is an understandable human trait. Less easy to understand is why so many views of the same flower or statue or church or citizen in native costume need to be shared with the world. Not always breathtaking either are several dozen slides of one's spouse standing in front of national monuments. ("Here we have Thelma standing in front of St. Peter's feeding the pigeons." Or, "This is a shot of George synchronizing his watch with Big Ben.")

More interesting, of course, is the spontaneous dialogue between spouses as they show the slides and disagree as to what a picture is, when it was taken, or even what country they were in at the time. Such dialogue avoids the most relevant question of all, Who cares? The answer, of course, is in the negative(s).

The deeper meaning of slide shows may not rest in the quality of the pictures or the commentary. After all, the intentions are good, even noble. People want to share with others the experiences which have meant much to them. They want to relive moments of importance, excitement, or meaning.

In this sense authentic religion is like a slide show: We want to share that which is full of vitality and adventure.

Yet, also like a slide show, authentic religion—particularly the Christian faith—is intensely personal. It can't be lived or experienced by one person *for* another person. We simply have to take the trip ourselves.

Heavenly Father, keep us from inflicting our private adventures on people who aren't interested. Watch over amateur photographers and their victims. And help us to experience your presence and accept no substitutes. In the name of him who showed us what you are like. AMEN.

16

On winter pleasures

Everyone knows that children love snow. The more there is of it, the better they like it. In fact, the joy that is felt at the sight of newly fallen snow is inversely proportional to the age of the beholder. For children, snow means outdoor sports, building snow persons, and possibly a vacation from school.

With the initial snowflake, some children immediately begin turning the dials to all local radio stations, trying to find one that is announcing the closing of schools. When they actually do close, most neighborhood children go over to the schoolyard and try to get into the gym to play basketball while others remain at home complaining to their mothers that they have nothing to do.

Adults look at snow differently than children. While it is theoretically true that nothing in nature is more beautiful than one snowflake, seldom do they come that way. From an adult perspective, the best thing that can be said of snow is that it makes one's own lawn look as nice as the neighbor's, but the beauty of a blanket of snow is always best appreciated by people with short driveways. As one philosopher, who is understandably unknown, put it: "More people would be satisfied with their walk in life if they didn't have to shovel it."

Many parents would modify the above statement to read: "More people would be satisfied with their children in winter if they didn't have to dress them warmly." A seven-year-old child, dressed for zero weather, is a modern marvel, a bona-fide study of the laws of thermodynamics and motion. By the time a child is dressed in long underwear, two pairs of pants, three pairs of socks, two sweaters, a heavy outercoat, a six-foot scarf, cap, earmuffs, and gloves, she is able to move with all the fluid grace of the well-dressed penguin she resembles. Chances are, furthermore, the child will announce, as the final knot in her scarf is tied, that she has to go to the bathroom. This is not often regarded as the best news of the hour, and it may explain why Eskimo families are quite small.

Once dressed, of course, the children will amuse themselves for several minutes by building snow forts, rolling over and over in the snow, and throwing snowballs at the postman. Occasionally, the small boy who hides within every adult male will come forth, and a well-intentioned father will take his children and their friends sledding. In reality, however, they take him for a ride, as the rituals of sledding with young boys and girls vary only slightly around the country.

For example, nearly every living person enjoys the sensation of gliding down a snow-padded hill on a sled. Few of those same people enjoy the walk back up the hill as much, and that climb is even less fun if one is pulling three sleds and two small children at the same time. The rides down get more thrilling as the children grow in courage. This is particularly true for father since it is difficult to steer a sled away from the tree at the bottom of the hill when most of the neighborhood children are stacked on his back and his cap has been shoved down over his face. Fortunately, the children manage to roll off the pile shortly before a collision occurs, and no one of any importance is crippled for life. In this way fathers are able to take one small step for parenthood and one giant, bone-crushing plop for Blue Cross.

The promise of hot chocolate and a roaring fire eventually triumph over the childish fun of putting snow down daddy's back, and the hopes of the indomitable snowdad for release from frostbite rise again. Stripped of approximately two tons of clothing, most of which is left dripping in the kitchen, and nestled in front of a roaring fire while young and old sip hot chocolate laced with marshmallows, lulled into a sense of peace by the crackling of the wood and the rhythmic sniffling of runny noses, all seems well with the world. That elusive treasure which we seek and find, only to lose and seek some more—a moment of joy—is experienced.

Nothing makes a person feel so much at home as a big snowstorm, and there may be no feeling quite so good as that of your own blood circulating through your body, bringing warmth and sensation back to the toes you thought were lost forever. There may be no closeness quite so intimate as that we feel when a child decides the right moment for snuggling has arrived. No food tastes so good as that particular cup of hot chocolate, and no entertainment ever provided by Hollywood or Las Vegas can match the silent joy of staring at a fire.

The experience is only temporary, of course. Someone has to mop the kitchen, hang up the clothes, wipe up the hot chocolate which boiled over on the stove, and clean the ashes out of the fireplace. Even so, it is worth the price, and it just may be that it takes cold weather to appreciate warm fires, walking uphill to make sliding downhill fun, and the routine of life to provide a background for its special moments.

The oldest news in the world is that life, like sledding, is full of ups and downs. Winter moments can be beautiful, and families should seize them when they can. For when winter comes, can influenza be far behind?

O God of the season, thanks for the snow and the sun which melts it, for children who help us see its value, and for tire chains which keep the school buses rolling. In the name of him who had the good fortune to live in a warm climate. AMEN.

17

On the day after Christmas

Probably no holiday, sacred or secular, generates so much anticipation as Christmas. After all, Christmas club savings accounts begin early in January, and merchandisers plan their advertising campaigns in July. Santa Claus arrives (frequently by helicopter) earlier each year, usually sometime between Halloween and Thanksgiving, and the months of November and December are saturated with jingles, TV commercials, and hard-sell promotions hawking the goodies of Christmas.

By the middle of December countless children have become convinced that their entire lives will be empty and meaningless if they do not possess by Christmas day a toy model of a supersonic thing that goes "glug-a-boom" and lights up on electronic command. Little children can't wait until Christmas arrives. Larger people, particularly parents of those little children, may be heard to utter the blasphemy of blasphemies: "I'll be glad when it's over!"

This is not, let it be made perfectly clear, because adults dislike the Yuletide season. Never, ever would such subversive statements escape from parental lips in the presence of children or tape recorders, for the wise parent

79

knows a sacred cow when he is gored by one. Experience has taught parents, however, that the reality of Christmas seldom, if ever, matches the expectations for it that the mythology about the season promotes.

Popular magazines, for example, picture a happy family sitting about a beautifully decorated tree, all wearing a beautific glow as they open in an orderly manner their gifts of love. Such magazines, however, do not usually portray the scene of one true-life Christmas in which a father overloaded the fireplace with wrapping paper, smoking the entire family out of the house and making a new paint job necessary.

Christmas dinner as illustrated in *Good Housekeeping* provides a scene not unlike Holy Communion, as three generations bow in prayer around a table loaded with turkey et al. Even the small children have their hands folded in prayer and nary a sibling is whispering or sneaking a piece of dressing with his fingers. Not pictured and often not even remembered (once again showing the power of the human psyche to repress unpleasantness) is the family dinner where egg nog was mistakenly used instead of milk in the turkey gravy. The gravy was therefore very strange, and the attendant results from eating it (and mixing with it in the tummy large quantities of chocolate Santas consumed earlier) will *never* be featured in any magazine save a medical journal.

Such experiences from real life cause veteran parents to anticipate Christmas primarily because it comes the day before their favorite holiday—the day after Christmas. By then, all the "D" batteries are mercifully dead.

The supersonic thing can no longer go "glug-a-boom," and the children are playing happily with the box it came in. The relatives have returned to their own homes, as happy to depart as their hosts were to see them leave. Meals for the next ten days are planned, as twelve pounds of leftover turkey and six cups of cranberry sauce can outlast any holiday season.

By then, you've given up hunting for the guarantee for the new electric blanket, philosophically assuming that it was burned along with the rest of the trash and the washing instructions for the cashmere sweater that, for the moment, fits perfectly. Also lost are the directions for the new game, "Kill the Enemy, a game for ages 6–60," which merely shows that the Lord works in mysterious ways, his wonders to perform.

The house is quiet, you've decided to leave the tree up for a week, and the moral obligation to sound "ho-ho-ho-ish" lies dormant for another year. The partridge is safely ensconced in the pear tree, and the little drummer boy has rub-a-dub-dubbed his last thumps for the season. Who knows? A husband and wife might even find time and opportunity for some friendly necking on the couch, just because they feel like it.

True, such descriptions of the day after Christmas can become as romanticized and sugar-coated as the holiday itself. Yet, December 26 or 27 has a great advantage over December 25, in that little is expected and, as a result, they often become serendipities—moments of unanticipated joy. Twentieth-century America puts so much burden on *the day* that there is little realistic hope that the reality can reflect the dream. The day after *the day* may therefore provide unexpected joys and unexpected contentment.

Who would have guessed it? But, then, who would have guessed that so much would have resulted from the birth of a mere baby born, of all places, in a manger?

O God, thank you for all the days you have given us. Help us to rejoice in each one and discover the holy day that awaits us. In the name of him who was a gift to all people. AMEN.

18

On chicken pox

Chicken pox is not a reason for writing a Greek tragedy. Everyone knows that childhood diseases come to all, regardless of race, creed, or color, and they probably belong with death and taxes as inevitables of life. When four children in one family experience chicken pox within a two-week span, however, that particular disease moves up in the rankings well past poison ivy and only slightly behind whooping cough.

Doctors, when contacted on the phone, are usually very helpful to the parent who is sure his children have entered the final stages of leprosy. They are able to identify the disease quickly from a description of the symptoms, and they provide comfort by announcing that "Chicken pox is really going around this year." After these words, you're on your own.

To be on your own means to turn to home remedy books, and many parents have learned to rely on veritable fountains of medical knowledge such as the *Medical and Health Encyclopedia (Illustrated)*. Listed below, for the benefit of other sufferers who have gone before and those yet to come, are helpful guidelines taken from real doctor books. Interpretive comments, intended to keep parents from laughing aloud, are also added.

(1) *"The best way to protect a child from chicken pox is to keep him away from other children who have the disease."* This advice is obviously helpful to large families and can best be followed by purchasing a new home complete with servants for every child. If this is not possible, preventive steps can be taken by removing all your children from school for the duration of the epidemic, hoping that chicken pox will not be going around next year when they repeat their grade levels.

(2) *"Children with chicken pox should not be permitted to go to school."* This wise counsel is happily followed by all children who catch chicken pox, especially since the disease usually produces only a mild fever and little nausea. The advice is not so well received by parents, usually mothers, who have long been this nation's keenest supporters of public schools for many reasons, a few of which have to do with education. Perceptive fathers will be sympathetic to the problems of having four itching children at home for two weeks, and the wisest of them will plan a lengthy business trip if at all possible.

Dedicated mothers will seek to entertain their children who, after the second day of watching soap operas, find themselves very bored. Thus, mothers play games with their speckled flock in the name of *passing time* and *expressing concern*. Monopoly, Scrabble, Flinch, Checkers, and Cribbage have their charm for both adults and children, but by the fourth day nobody really cares if you own *both* Boardwalk *and* Park Place with four hotels. Interlocking puzzles provide a change of pace, of course, causing what seemed like an eternity of time to be more like a life sentence in Sing Sing.

It is, in fact, during the fourth day of chicken pox that many mothers experience a related illness known best by its nonscientific name, "cabin fever." The primary symptoms are glassy-eyed stares and occasional incoherent mumbling to oneself. Those mothers whose husbands have gone on business trips also fantasize a great deal, often laughing aloud at thoughts of violence and demonstrating unnatural interest in E.R.A.

(3) *"When a child has chicken pox, the chief factors in treatment are diet and the care of the skin. The diet is usually mild and soft. Mild, warm baths are used."* Ice cream, jello, and puddings are mild and soft, and they usually taste good to sick children. By the fifth day, however, pudding has lost much of its culinary delight for parents who have felt morally obligated to eat what their children have been eating. Dedicated parents, nonetheless, will share the same menu with good humor, forbearance, and late night raids on the refrigerator after the children are alseep.

Mild, warm baths are of considerable help, too, especially to the parents. They are also appreciated by the children with chicken pox. In fact, homemade treatments make the bathing experience for children particularly fascinating. Bathing a child with wet oatmeal, a treatment with mysterious powers even modern science fails to understand, eases the itching considerably although one never has the same taste for Quaker Oats at breakfast again.

(4) *"Make certain that the child does not scratch the spots, as there is danger of secondary infection."* While this is clearly a noble goal, reaching it when four children are itching at the same time requires eternal vigilance. It also requires that the children wear gloves from morning til night, have metal tubes fastened to their elbows so that they cannot bend their arms, and other measures be taken that make the Marquis de Sade sound like the father of the year. The children by this time itch as much as Job sitting on his dung heap and look something like the Plantom of the Opera.

Fortunately, there proves to be life after chicken pox. There even turn out to be some unexpected, happy results beyond the crusts and scabs of the disease. The children are nearly as joyful to return to school as their mothers are to see them go. Kids who have missed school because of chicken pox, it turns out, are treated as status figures by their peers, and many a recovered child will gleefully relate how he got to eat ice cream *every* day and point with pride to the remaining marks of his illness.

Parents rejoice in the fact that once you've had chicken pox, it almost never returns. Very few problems in life go away forever, so it is a good idea to celebrate those which are never recycled. After all, arguments are repeated again and again. Promises are made, broken, made, and broken again. We make mistakes and live to make them again.

Not so with chicken pox. It has no reruns. If more of life could be like chicken pox, would it be better? We wonder . . .

No, thanks, Lord, once is enough. AMEN.

19

On Valentine's Day

Whoever made February the shortest month of the year certainly knew what he was doing. The charm of winter has melted by the middle of February, even if its dirty gray drifts have not. The pleasant dispositions of saints and sinners alike have been sorely tested by the common cold at this stage of the winter, and many of us discover that February is the month which all those first payments don't begin until.

No wonder Valentine's Day comes when it does. If there were not a special day set aside to honor love and romance in February, we might yield to the temptation to join the ground hogs (an appropriate mascot for the month) and disappear from sight until March.

Fortunately, February 14 appears on schedule every year, and not a moment too soon. It reminds us that while life is simply one darn thing after another, love is two darned things after each other. It instills in young and old a renewed sense of romance at a time when even your libido has chilblains.

For once we can be grateful to commercialism, for were it not for the candy, flower, and underwear salesmen of the world, we would have only two dead presidents and a bashful groundhog to celebrate. The ads and the promotions, however, do their work and raise our romantic consciousness so that tenderness and affection, while not running rampant, do more than lie there like soggy cereal. A husband may notice that his wife no longer reminds him to fasten his seat belt, and she may suddenly become aware that he forgot absent-mindedly to peck her goodbye when he left for the office yesterday.

Their children may also remind them that romance is not dead but only gone to Florida for the winter. They do this by exchanging valentines with every child in their classes, treating everyone the same except for the thirty or forty who are "true loves." Special recipients will receive preferential treatment, such as a box of heart-shaped, homemade cookies with pink icing which are wrapped and delivered in a snowstorm by a long-suffering father to a six-year-old boy friend who had beaned his true love with a snowball at recess the day before. The small, seven-year-old daughter, of course, is too shy to deliver the valentine cookies to the boy's house herself, so she hides in the car while dad plays delivery-person. The homemade cookies, after having been dropped a couple of times, appear to be the product of a broken home, but the cause of romance is served as adults remember that snow on the roof means it's time to build a fire in the furnace.

Thus, many husbands seek creative ways to say "I love you" to their brides of twenty years or more. True, the regular methods of passionate expression are still effective and lots of fun, but romantics coming out of hibernation plan special gestures to decorate the occasion. A few husbands create their own valentines and send innovative greetings, such as "May I be your Groundhog of Happines on Valentine's Day?" Other husbands, delirious with self-confidence, may purchase an exotic card and send it to their wives with an anonymous note: "After all these years, I still can't forget that night!"

Tokens of affection, necessarily small because the income tax refund has not yet arrived, are sometimes exchanged. Careful shoppers discover gifts of love that will last forever, such as fossil imprints that are over a million years old and start at one dollar each. Hare Krishna incense comes in strawberry and pineapple scents, costs only fifty-nine cents for twelve cones, and is guaranteed either to kindle romance or suggest fruit salad for supper. Such gifts, when presented in a shopping bag from the most expensive store in town, are heartfelt demonstrations that you cared enough to deliver gifts in the very best.

Even less expensive and probably more romantic are tender moments of memory that only you and she have shared, such as dancing in the living room with the lights down low to records you've collected over the years. The tenderness of such moments is rich and full, rising above the fact that Perry Como's voice loses its romantic tone when the record skips three grooves a minute. Back rubs and foot massages are gestures of romance that only happily married people fully appreciate, and some couples have feet that require more appreciation and more happy marriedness than others.

90

We jest, of course, and yet we don't. Many articles are written every year which focus on the need to keep romance alive in marriage, possibly because they need to be written. Perhaps every marriage has its Februarys, and it needs its Valentine's Days as well. Still, if two people care deeply for each other in the first place and if they can affirm their middle-aged version of that love twenty years later, their marriage will survive nearly any catastrophe that awaits them, even the snickers of their children who catch them dancing in the dark.

Creator God, thank you for the feelings of romance and passion which continue to flow through our bodies, even as our arteries harden and our veins become varicose. Some of us, Lord, have no complaints about this part of life. In the name of him who blessed marriage at Cana of Galilee. AMEN.

20

On parent-teacher conferences

There was a time when parents were asked to visit school only when there had been an accident, such as when your son fell off the parallel bars and bled on the hardwood floor. Or they were called when there had been trouble, illustrated by the time your ten-year-old daughter placed a tack on the chair of her fourth-grade teacher, an action which led to a sudden uprising.

Today it is different. All parents are invited to visit school for regular conferences, and the opportunity to see and know those who are shaping the minds of your own flesh and blood is one to be grasped—especially if the parent has the vague and uneasy feeling that his child is highly motivated during recess and no other time. The feeling is vague because a parent has only his child's report card on which to make a judgment, and no one can understand a modern report card.

Modern report cards measure a child according to the statistical averages of a certain age group and by his study habits, if there are any. The criteria are always couched in educational jargon which are words that describe commonplace events in unclear ways. (Example:

"Martha relates well to peers during coordinated recreational activities." Translation: "She doesn't cheat much at kickball during recess.")

Hence, the parent-teacher conference has come to assume an important place in family life. Parents have a chance to find out if their child is going to be promoted to the next grade since her report card only said that "an enrichment program was indicated," and that could mean either "smart" or "dumb." The conferences also provide occasion to deliver messages to the teacher that a mere signature at the bottom of the cards could never convey, for example, "Our Ruthie is a sensitive child and you shouldn't have yelled at her just because she glued two erasers together."

Teachers, however, usually control discussion in such conferences, and they probably spend hours at educational institutes memorizing new jargon in which to cloak their real feelings toward some pupils that otherwise must be repressed because of possible lawsuits. (At one gathering of teachers, the question was allegedly asked: "If reincarnation is true, in what form would you choose to return to life?" Twenty-seven percent listed "A childhood disease.")

Thus, a teacher will calmly chat with a parent and say that "Sarah exhibits a resentment of obligations which would appear to stem from environmental influences." In English this means: "Why didn't you teach your kid to hang up her coat and brush her teeth, Mrs. Slob?" Or, "Bret adjusts well to his peer group, but he seems to be lacking in reading readiness." When translated, this means

93

your son would much rather look at the pictures in the book than read such fascinating dialogue as "Run, Dick run. See Dick run."

In such conferences it is possible to have ominous-sounding evaluations explained, so that parents can find out whether their child is merely going through phase number thirty-four or headed resolutely toward a life of crime. For example, the note your daughter brought home from school said: "Martha offers a paradox in that she seems unable to relate to current events. There is danger that she may develop misplaced values." Conversation with the teacher eventually indicates that Martha can remember Pete Rose's batting average from day to day but thinks President Ford is a Democrat.

Indeed, if parents attend enough conferences with the teachers of their children, the cause of American education will be greatly served. Personal, trusting relationships may be established between parent and teacher, and real communication will occur. (Teacher: "Bret's interest inventory is deficient. Yet he appears to possess an exhibitionistic compulsion to demonstrate his masculinity." Parent: "You mean he gets bored and then belts Roger with his lunch box?" Teacher: "You guessed 'er, Chester!")

School days are not always good old golden rule days. In competitive America where success is graded early, children quickly learn that adults place high value on what is achieved in school. In some ways this is good, for each child does have a potential to achieve something that can bring a sense of satisfaction. Modern education

94

rewards a greater variety of gifts, skills, and talents than it once did, too, and this is genuine progress.

Even so, in school—as in the rest of life—there is the hidden danger that a child will feel worthless if marks are poor or acceptance into somebody's accelerated reading program does not come. A crucial question for parents trying to be Christian is this: Are our children under-achievers, or are we overexpecters?

We need to remember that we are saved by grace and not by works. Our task is to help children know they are O.K. They are loved as they are. If parents and teachers can help a child know he is accepted by God and by adults, the grace of God will be experienced even when it isn't explained. The truth is that God loves us even if we don't make the top reading group.

O Great Teacher, help us not to think of you as the Great Record-Keeper in the sky. Free us to learn as best we can and rejoice in the results. In the name of him who taught us how to pray. AMEN.

21

On spring fervor

Spring always comes when we need it most. The best
evidence we have for needing spring is the way we greet
it before it fully arrives. At the first sign of a warm day
in March, college students will flop on the nearest dry
turf and try to tan their goose pimples. Car owners will
drain the antifreeze from the automobile two weeks too
soon, and children will run in and out of the house, slam-
ming the doors they left open all winter. At last, we think,
the flowers will come up and the heating bill go down.

So eager are most of us to escape the claustrophobia
of winter, we temporarily forget that the season brings
other urges in addition to the desire to fly a kite, run
through the rain, or kiss your wife on the back of the
neck. In fact, kissing one's wife on the back of her neck
may cause her to dust the ceiling with her eyes, and the
first rumblings that it is time to clean the house begin to
stir. Middle-aged people are particularly vulnerable to
such urges, as most of us had strict toilet training as children. Some of us also had mothers for whom cleanliness
was only a fleck of dust away from godliness, and cobwebs
were an offense against the Creator.

Thus, a transformation in perspective can occur quicker than a change in the weather. We experience the difference between saying, "You look like the coming of spring," and commenting, "You look like the end of a hard winter." The inevitable result is that romance is transcended by reality, and spring fever is supplanted by spring fervor.

Impulses to clean always begin either with the attic or the basement, a mindset probably associated with the phrase, "We cleaned the house from top to bottom." Cleaning either place is less fun than going to a circus although many basements appear to have been lived in by elephants. It is not difficult, in fact, to perceive the enormous problems in building a better world when we finally get around to cleaning out the attic. In this experience we learn how important it is to get rid of other people's "junk" while preserving our own "precious goods" without which the quality of life would surely suffer.

Families which are run essentially as dictatorships, a form of government for which many fathers have secretly longed, do not have to face the dilemmas of those families where democracy has gained a foothold. It would be easier if a father/husband would be the sole arbiter of what goes and what stays, for, while fairness might not always reign, the attic might eventually get cleaned.

As it is, we end up keeping most of the things we never use but might should things happen differently than they ever have before. In the process of trying to clear out some of life's debris, we experience the phenomenon of rearrangement, which is something like trying to bail out a bathtub while the faucet is still running. The following conversation may illustrate the point:

WIFE *(holding large Goodwill bag):* How about getting rid of this old wool sweater?

HUSBAND *(grabbing it from her hands):* That's my tennis sweater!

WIFE: But you don't play tennis any more. You haven't played tennis in five years.

HUSBAND: Yes, but if I ever do, I'll have a tennis sweater, won't I? It's a long-term investment.

Garages and basements attract old and unread books like a magnet, and they become depositories for things which are only examined in the annual discussion about whether or not to get rid of them. An old *Home Medical Guide* may be kept even though most of the diseases it describes have been eradicated and its treatments border on voodoo. Rock collections which your teenager gathered in grade school suddenly assume value considerably greater than gold and only slightly less than sugar.

Toys that were rejected the day after Christmas become fascinating to small children ten minutes before they would otherwise have gone into the bag (Note: the toys, not the children). Cleaning an attic is fundamentally the task of deciding between sentiment and sediment, and in those families where the members have a voice, the reasons of the heart almost always triumph over the logic of space and neatness.

Perhaps we will be better off if we treat the annual

assault on the basement or attic as a ritual rather than a necessity. Remembering is good for people, and the souvenirs of the past may be therapeutic reminders. A man's letter sweater which still fits is probably equal in value to an hour on a psychiatrist's couch. Boxes of old love letters are often better reading than the latest novel, and what one stores in an attic may tell more about that person than a Rorschach test.

We do well to remember that our storage places are filled full of things we couldn't bear to throw away, and one person's junk is another person's treasure. The ritual of rearrangement may keep us honest and force us to decide whether last year's valuables are this year's expendables. People seeking to live Christian lives ought to do this regularly, too, for where our treasures are, there will our hearts be as well.

All-seeing God, help us to discern what is treasure and what is junk, both in our attics and in our lives. In the name of him who called us to compare treasure on earth with treasure in heaven. AMEN.

22

On paper routes

Delivering newspapers has long been regarded as the first step in the free-enterprise system. Indeed, the newspaper boy is the prototype of the system, the Horatio Alger of each new generation, the living evidence that hard work and self-discipline will be rewarded with well-built character and approximately three dollars a week.

Parents of deliverers of newspapers have maximum respect for this phase of the capitalistic system. While most Americans take their morning papers for granted, evidently assuming that they are delivered by the tooth fairy or regurgitated by the welcome mat, the families of newspaper-persons know differently. In fact, in perhaps no other business are so many housewives, college teachers, corporation executives, and government officials moonlighting, all because their children have paper routes. The hard truth is that when a child assumes a paper route, his father or mother assumes one, too.

It was not so intended. The parents, especially those who were once paper-persons themselves but whose memories have begun to fail, think a paper route will teach their son or daughter courtesy and responsibility (as well as provide an argument against an increase in allowance!). What they overlook are certain brutal facts such as the discovery that morning papers are delivered rather early in the day.

The child's early rising builds character, but father or mother, whose character is not only already built but probably beginning to depreciate, does not usually feel the need for such ongoing edification. However, alarm clocks, sirens, or automatic radios seem ineffective in getting a youthful paper-person out of bed at approximately 4:30 A.M. so that the latest record of yesterday's murders and corruption can be enjoyed (three hours later!!) with one's morning coffee. Seemingly, only a parent motivated by a high purpose—namely, overwhelming resentment—is able to propel the product of his planned parenthood out of the pad.

Parents also get the opportunity to suffer from all the childhood diseases again, as their children's skin rashes, colds, and diarrhea force the adults to take their places and venture out into the night, the snow, and the rain to deliver the news of the day. Humiliation is added to suffering when the parent discovers he can't deliver papers as well as his children. Most kids are able to lob a paper thirty feet and have it land at least near the porch. Parents, on the other hand, end up spending considerable time retrieving papers from shrubs, trees, and eavetroughs. Some, in fact, are never found again, or at least not until the spring thaws expose last winter's paper which landed in a snow-covered flowerbed in a neighbor's yard.

Such problems, whether created by parent or child,

inevitably lead to further adventures. Persons whose papers arrived late or not at all often call the home of the delivery person. Probably the callers are human beings who are nice to their mothers and kind to animals, but evidently failure to deliver a paper on time or in excellent condition is a crime second only to treason and far ahead of extortion. Such persons have been known to speak their complaints crisply into the telephone, occasionally even making references to one's mental capacities in the process.

Parents, who almost always are the ones to receive such calls, apologize profusely and sacrifice their own copy of the *Daily Blah* by sending it over immediately. This usually satisfies the customer but also limits the family to reading the only paper that is left, the one that fell into a sewer and was rescued by the family dog.

What's a parent to do? Well, he can read his Bible, and many passages take on new meaning, especially those dealing with enemies and rejection. He can rejoice in the fact that he and his son or daughter will have a closer relationship than most, as hardship and pain build such bonds. Parents and children both will grow in self-control and patience, lessons best learned as they try for the fourteenth time to collect from the neighborhood grouch who is sure he already paid. A child's values will be formed and shaped, too, as money will not be deemed nearly important enough to warrant so much hardship. Mainly, however, the generation gap will be bridged, and a great tradition will be kept intact. For an important truth will continue to be passed from parent to child, the

102

one which begins with those immortal words: "When I was your age . . ."

O God, who watches over paper-people before dawn and on collection day, grant patience and forbearance to their families. Stay customers from taking out their frustrations on children who come to collect. May papers land on the porch and not break any windows. In the name of him who was the bringer of Good News. AMEN.

23

On children in their natural habitats

Psychologists tell us that every person needs space to call his own. All humans require "turf" for which they can assume ownership and responsibility. Children, having some similarity to real persons, have their needs for space, too, and often it is a significant moment in the life of a family when the signs and symbols of ownership first appear.

Initially, parents enthusiastically cooperate in the venture. Mothers may go shopping with their daughters for curtains and matching bedspreads. Fathers build bookshelves and hang cork bulletin boards, whistling while they work. Sooner than they expect, however, parental identification with that section of the house disappears.

If, as the poet says, a man's home is his castle, what is a child's room? Many parents would conclude it is a unique combination of urban slum and a chamber of horrors. Most of them have all the earmarks of an eyesore. Each child's room or, if a room is shared with others, each child's corner of a room, soon becomes "distinctive," which means it is like visiting a foreign country whenever an adult musters the courage to enter.

"Distinctiveness" is achieved by careful selection of decorative materials. Posters of movie stars, athletes, and rock musicians nearly cover the wallpaper a parent shopped four days to find that matched the rug that is shoved under the bed. Alan Alda and Robert Redford seem decent enough, but Alice Cooper hanging by a rope and bleeding through the eyes would not be an adult choice for greeting each morning. Nor does a black revolving light which makes one's pajamas transparent allow a parent to feel at home in the child's room—or in this century, for that matter.

Most parents recognize the right of children to express their own tastes and protect their own privacy. Young people have a way of hinting at those rights by posting subtle signs on their doors such as "DO NOT ENTER" or "DEATH TO ALL INVADERS." Should a parent dare to enter the room, adjust his vision to the strobe lights, fight off the nausea induced by burning incense, and gaze about, the real reason for the warning signs quickly becomes apparent. The "NO TRESPASSING" signs do not indicate a wider-than-usual generation gap. They are simply early warnings to health inspectors and sanitation engineers.

Small children are often hoarders with bad memories. Months after a tenth birthday, a slice of cake may be found neatly wrapped in cellophane and moulding in the sock drawer. Treasures of jelly beans hide among the handkerchiefs, and cookie crumbs are the natural bedmates of small boys and girls who like to eat themselves to sleep.

Older children put their apple cores in the wastebaskets which are regularly emptied every other month. Whereas adults and other persons from outer space are carefully screened before entering, dogs, cats, guinea pigs, and gerbils are not only welcomed, they are frequently granted long-term visas. Animals, unlike parents, do not make moral judgments about the sanitary condition of a room, and six weeks of dirty underwear provide excellent sleeping accommodations for the average middle-class dog.

It is because of such circumstances as these that cleaning up one's room becomes a point of contention between parents and their children. Whereas "go to your room" was once a command of discipline for a child, such visits today cause us to wonder whether Job would have complained about his dung heap had he been fourteen years old. Parental prayers are uttered: "Lord, where have we failed this time?" Ultimatums are issued: "You *will* put clean sheets on your bed even if these have not been 'slept up' yet!" Children respond by hiding junk under the bean bag chair or by sleeping in their clothes on top of their neatly made beds for two weeks. Eventually, war is declared or negotiations carried out so that the issue is finally resolved temporarily one more time forever.

It may be that such confrontations *must* occur as children move toward adulthood. Even in those rare homes where neat children keep tidy rooms, those same siblings will find ways of doing battle with their parents and asserting their independence. Those adults who claim, years later, that "our children never gave us a minute's trouble" probably mean that they had hours and days of it instead.

The parent who seeks to raise responsible children will help them by engaging in the conflict: children *should* clean up their rooms! Even so, it helps to remember that it is not like real war where everybody loses. It is the "lamb's war" wherein sheep and lion lie down together and a balance of freedom and responsibility are won. Knowing this will probably not get a messy room cleaned any sooner, but it may enable parents to face Alice Cooper with a smile.

O Lord, help us never to confuse cleanliness with godliness. Nevertheless, spare us from more clutter than we can stand. In the name of him who dignified a manger. AMEN.

24

On Father's Day

No man can pretend to speak for all fathers, but it is safe to say that middle-aged men generally want the same things on Father's Day—that special time invented by the socks and necktie people to exploit the guilt feelings of wives and children all over America. Hence, this essay is loaded with advice to wives and children on what to give to fathers on their day, especially to men like this writer who do not smoke, drink, play golf, or care very much how he smells.

First, please honor the fact we are set in our ways. Most of us who are now reaching middle-age and have several children are beginning to suffer from milestones. As a result we have decided we do not want to wear pants with wide legs and huge cuffs even if all the movie stars, professional athletes, and sexy Europeans in the world wear them.

We assume, after all, that our daughters must have some grudging appreciation for our taste in clothes, as they have confiscated many of our T-shirts, sweat shirts, and bulky sweaters for their own wardrobes. We don't really mind giving up our narrow neckties to our sons since using them as tails for their kites made them the envy of the neighborhood, but we ask you not to replace them with a gift of those enormous wide, wool ties that give one the feeling of wearing a horse blanket about his neck. Some of us are glad we don't live in this day and age, so give us back our clothes.

Secondly, forgive us our trespasses. Fathers in particular carry considerable guilt about being gone so much, or for being inadequate father-figures, or for losing their tempers for bad reasons. We know you want our time and energy, and we are happy to give it to you as soon as football, basketball, and baseball seasons are over. We know you want our attention and we know you love us, but we often don't manage to be the strong, self-giving paragons your mothers—our wives—have led you to believe we are. Some of the time we're just tired and deliberately neglect our fatherly responsibilities. We'd just like to lie around and fight tooth decay with our eyes closed.

Fortunately, most of us in our family circumstances long ago gave up many of our pretenses, realizing that standing on dignity around our children makes for very poor footing. We're anxious about our responsibilities, and yet we're never quite certain when to be tough and when to be tender. So, please forgive us for our forthright indecision, our occasional laziness, and our tendency to mount the family soapbox for colorful orations at the drop of a problem.

Thirdly, we'd like some gratitude for one thing we've done for you children, which is the nicest thing anybody could have done: we married your mothers in the first

109

place. Please note the natural order of these relationships—our wives were our wives before they were your mothers. Whatever subtle commentary this has for the "new morality," it also means that we have certain desires to be alone with them, to have adult conversations with them, and once in awhile to leave you behind feeling rejected while we go out to dinner. More often, however, we'd like to spend a quiet evening at home on the couch, which is about all we have left to spend after paying for your braces, music lessons, allergy shots, and book fees.

Finally, as a gift to dad on Father's Day, don't change too much. If you were perfect children, we'd have to be perfect fathers, and we've already made our confession on that score. If you never interrupted us, we'd be unable to appreciate uninterrupted conversation for the priceless gift it is. If you didn't fail in what you attempt from time to time, we'd miss out on a father's special moment, the chance to hold his son or daughter and say, "It's O.K. We still love you." If you weren't capable of doing some things well, we'd miss out on the most pleasurable of all original sins—fatherly pride in the achievements of his children. In fact, if you weren't the way you are, we'd never have learned the difference between calamities and mild vexations which is one of the most important distinctions life has to offer.

So, don't trouble yourselves to shop for expensive gifts which you'll use your lunch money to purchase, as you did last year. Vintage fathers have their full complement of wives and children without which we wouldn't even qualify for Dad's Day, and one more wide tie and a pair

110

of spotted undershorts will only be extra proof of what we already know—we're loved by you very much.

O God, whom we call Father, thank you for wives and children without whom our status as fathers would be impossible. Help us to manage two contradictory tasks: first, to help our children reach their goals and, second, to accept them as they are. In the name of him who showed us you are like a Father, only better. AMEN.

25

On church youth groups

Between the innocence of kindergarten and the indifference of early adulthood exist many stages of Christian growth, some of which are positive. Little children, for example, usually love Sunday school, and millions of bulletin boards, cupboard doors, and refrigerators are decorated with drawings and finger paintings brought home to mommy. Older grade-school children, especially young boys, often have their destructive impulses sublimated in Sunday school, and they usually learn to stack the pieces after they've destroyed the furniture.

Where the youth group fits into God's cosmic scheme of things, however, is not so clear. Uncertainty first rears its timid head when one notices that the number of youth who are physically present at meetings often represents only a fraction of those, as they say in churches, "on the roll." Small doubts may even reach rampant skepticism when attempts at communication indicate that many youth are present only in the sense that they are not elsewhere.

This is not to say, let the record show, that all the MYF's, BYF's, GYF's, and FYF's in the world are poorly attended or mere gathering places for spiritual zombies. The problem is the gap between what adult church people think a YF should be and what, in fact, one usually is. Parents often want the faith sustained, the Bible learned, and positive behavior patterns for life established, all without messing up the basement. In other words, adults basically have nothing against young people. They just don't want their child to become one.

Parental nostalgia about their own youth groups is plentiful. "In the days when we were young people"—the history lesson begins—"we never missed youth meeting." That memory may be accurate, as in rural and small-town America youth meeting was a social occasion, a gathering place approved by parents where meetings began with prayer and ended with softball games. Many teenagers of today will say the same thing about their youth meetings as they look back upon them. Most youth do not attend and they don't seem to miss them, either.

Thus, those parents who inwardly hope that the Sunday evening youth meeting will redeem their children from the Pit have a different set of expectations than their teenagers. In most communities there are better opportunities for recreation than a church youth program provides although the many trips to amusement parks that are held in the name of Christ show that adults keep trying. Certainly, too, the old format of "studying a lesson" in youth meeting has fallen on hard times, as boys and girls will study all week but never on Sunday.

What's a dedicated, conscientious, concerned, loving Christian parent who wants his kids out of the house on

113

Sunday evening to do? No easy answers present themselves, but one can get a clue by looking at those infrequent situations in which several young people, minds and all, are clearly enthusiastic about being together, even when religion is the topic under discussion. When such happens, the common denominator usually does not turn out to be the fanciness of the facilities, the marvelousness of the materials, or even the bounty of the budget. Usually the answer is in the people—adults who like and enjoy young people and who get liked and enjoyed in return.

This is not to say that the beatific vision pictured on the covers of the denominational youth magazines is ever fully experienced. Young people seldom metamorphize like caterpillars into butterflies, shedding their adolescence before the very eyes of the youth leader. More often than not, youth meetings are encounters with chaos, and any adults who work with them probably have masochistic tendencies.

Youth leaders must be young enough to recover from pneumonia incurred after being sprayed by gleeful teenagers at the annual car wash. They must feign joy at the thought of sleeping on the ground on the way to the work camp where they will acquire blisters doing tasks they neglected to do at home because they went to the work camp. Knowing something about God and the Christian religion are also helpful, especially those parts having to do with inadequacy.

Indeed, knowing something about the Christian faith is crucial, although not in the sense we normally think. A good analogy for "faith" is "risk" or "adventure," and such words aptly describe most youth meetings. Young people are cutting umbilical cords right and left during their teen years, and many days they feel and think first like adults and then like children. They crave individual attention, yet long desperately to be part of a group. They're easily embarrassed, yet delight in life's embarrassments—especially those happening to their adult sponsors. They are in the process of discovering that the weaker sex is really the stronger sex because of the weakness of the stronger sex for the weaker sex. Even so, some of them figure out for themselves what the Christian religion has to do with all this.

With good fortune and pizza parties after the meeting as a bribe, a portion of the Christian religion may be absorbed. Equally important, however, will be the feeling that youth sometimes have when they're with their peers in such meetings, namely, a sense of security about being a part of the church. They feel accepted in spite of their awkwardness, forgiven in the face of foolishness, and taken seriously in the middle of teasing.

No one knows whether this really occurs or is merely the wishful thinking of youth leaders grasping for a reason to justify their existence. Either way, church youth groups will probably survive and may do some good. Some of the young people will undoubtedly grow up and become adult sponsors themselves, thereby learning the one fact of youth work about which all adult leaders agree: "When we were your age, we were younger."

Eternal God, steadfastly protect youth groups and their

leaders from the worst impulses of each. Grant patience and strong lungs to adult sponsors, and to youth give some small inclination to pay attention. In the name of him whose teenage years are not recorded in the Bible. AMEN.

26

On buying automobiles

For most Americans the automobile is much more than a conveyance for getting from here to there. Buying, trading, repairing, washing, waxing, and admiring cars tell us more about our hidden selves than all the psychiatrists and all the mothers-in-law in the world.

Most obvious is the use of the car as a status symbol. Big cars generally are driven by Important People, while little cars are owned by less important people or politicians wanting to appear humble. Intellectuals drive foreign-made cars, and the obscurity of the model is directly related to professorial rank of the owner. Sports cars are driven by persons who represent a cross section of social and economic classes in America, their common denominator being the ability to enjoy riding in a machine that travels ninety miles an hour six inches off the ground!

Rather than status, however, sports cars allegedly reveal our sexual fantasies and hidden drives. Middle-aged men, psychologists say, often buy sleek, fast, *red* sports cars because they are beginning to harbor fears about their virility, and such machines compensate for this anxiety. Middle-aged men with four or more children, of course, buy station wagons, as they want nothing more to do with virility.

For nearly all car-buyers, the actual process of purchasing any model at any price exposes his (or her) sinfulness as effectively as the apple trapped Adam and Eve. Like them, we want the best of all possible worlds—without conditions—and yet we can't resist the temptations that blow the whole deal.

Thus, we go to the dealer to buy an automobile that gets good mileage, promises low maintenance, carries six people comfortably, rides smoothly, will do seventy-five miles per hour, has a two-year guarantee, costs little, and will impress the neighbors. The salesman (that is, tempter) has just what we want at a price we can afford. What he also has that we didn't know we wanted, at prices we can't afford, are "extras."

To be sure, the word *extras* requires definition as buyer and seller do not always share a common understanding of that term. Naive car-buyers assume that such items as the transmission, the front seats, and the taillights would be "standard." That they are, of course, unless the words *automatic, bucket,* and *back-up* appear respectively before those other terms. Then they become "extras" (translation: cost a lot more).

The salesmen, however, know their way around the garden. They know that grown men secretly long for air conditioning, automatic windows, and tinted glass. They also know that wives (nee: Eve) admire interiors that look like homes, that teenagers feel deprived without automatic tape decks, and that small children don't care what's on a car so long as it's orange or red. By the time all those participants in the process have finished influencing each other, a car has been purchased that meets everybody's needs—particularly the financial ones of the dealer or salesman. They are now "owners," an inaccurate figure of speech referring to people who have made small down payments and assumed large debts at high interest rates from friendly lending institutions. Like Adam and Eve, they have their garden of delights, the only difference being that they drive away in it.

Buying automobiles tells us primarily what we can afford. It is axiomatic that we can afford what we want, and we cannot afford what we do not want. We approve of simplicity and frugality, and so we rationalize our extravagance by eating peanut butter sandwiches for lunch on Mondays and washing the car (that is, idol) ourselves.

What's an American car-buying, consumer-oriented Christian to do? The answers, clearly, are unclear. Certainly, the question must be asked, for Jesus instructed us to seek first his kingdom and his righteousness, and other things could come later. Our task, therefore, is to make sure we do not treat that which is essential as only an extra. It is probably best that the meek will inherit the earth, for no one else can afford car payments.

O God, thank you for accepting us as we are, whether

119

we drive big cars or little ones. Help us not to yield unto temptation, especially at car-buying time. In the name of him who warned us about earthly treasures that rust. AMEN.

27

On acquiring a driver's license

No event in the life of an American teenager carries greater significance than acquiring a driver's license. It is a rite of passage into a new world, for the automobile in our society stands for Adulthood. For better or worse— and there is usually lots of each—the keys to the ignition are the keys to the kingdom in the minds of young people.

The American life-style conditions youth to think in these terms. Children in grade school vicariously gain status by volunteering their parents' services as chauffeurs for school events. Kids are hauled everywhere by automobile, so often, in fact, that small boys think their pants are held up by seat belts and fear they will lose them when they get out of the car. The day a new car is purchased by a family is almost as exciting as the day a new baby is born, although easier on the mother. Little boys collect toy cars and can identify make, model, and year of big ones before they can recite the multiplication tables. Toy cars are the seeds of *machismo*—the need of males to assert their masculinity—and they are planted early in American boys.

The day inevitably arrives when a son or daughter

announces cheerfully at breakfast that next term's courses will include driver's training. While such programs of instruction are supposed to teach new drivers how to avoid all the bad techniques old drivers have taken years to learn, the hidden intent is clearly psychological. Few parents can emotionally handle the mental picture of their sixteen-year-old son or daughter, who still has acne, backing the family car out of the driveway into traffic. Backing a school-leased car into traffic under the supervision of a highly trained instructor who sits poised behind the dual controls that provide fail-safe guarantees against disaster—that vision, while not heavenly, can be appropriated without chest pains if sufficient black coffee is at hand.

Parents, long accustomed to looking for silver linings in the dark clouds of child-rearing, may even convince themselves that there are benefits in having another driver in the family. In their mind's eye they see older sisters delivering and collecting younger ones, while they drink coffee at home. The vision of cross-town errands run by a new driver eager to navigate the family car seems positively heart-warming. They may, if the coffee is strong enough, contemplate the thought of having a new partner in keeping the car clean, changing the oil, and sharing in gasoline costs.

Such fantasies are destroyed long before parents enter psychosis and shortly after the driver's training course begins. It turns out that driver education in your school includes only six hours of actual road experience, most of which is spent learning to parallel park unsuccessfully.

Your youngster still expects to practice in the family car and wants you to help her learn to drive. This experience, sorrowfully, leads to a violation of one's own self-image —that of an understanding, patient, and calm human being. Father Jekyll suddenly becomes Mr. Hyde, as the inability of a novice driver to place a car in gear or the tendency to run over the curb while turning corners causes screaming, pounding the dashboard, and the consumption of six rolls of Tums. Going down a one-way street the wrong way proves to be an effective attention-getting mechanism, as are the jerky starts and stops for which beginning drivers are famous and from which medical interest in whiplash first arose.

Research shows that children turn out to be about as safe drivers as their parents, thereby fulfilling the Scripture that the sins of fathers are visited upon later generations. The total meaning of the experience, however, does not have to be grasped to discover its significance. Not only does a driver's license mean entrusting control of a powerful machine to a child-adult, it also represents a *loss* of control by a parent over a child—if such existed in the first place.

Personal responsibility ceases to be a figure of speech and becomes a matter of life and death. Concern for others quickly becomes more than an expression used in Sunday school; it describes a series of deeds that have cause-and-effect consequences. In short, learning how to drive displays a microcosm of real life where morality and faith assume the form of tangible acts.

Most young people rise to the occasion and acquire,

not only a license, but also a sense of responsibility. Most parents survive the learning period with only a temporary nervous tick and live to rejoice in the new freedom and maturity they helped their children acquire. They may even resolve to be better drivers themselves, thereby reducing the odds of drawing upon the higher insurance rates they must now pay.

Ever-present God, help us to be safe drivers and responsible persons. Help parents keep their cool when their children are driving the new, partially-paid-for family car. In the name of him who was concerned for the highways and byways of life. AMEN.

28

On night people in the morning

For many years early rising has been regarded as a sign of godliness. Really good Catholics always go to early mass, and really good Protestants never miss the Easter sunrise service more than once a year, and they usually feel pangs of guilt when they do. Indeed, William Cowper, an eighteenth-century hymn writer, represents what many Christians even today regard as the proper model of self-discipline, preferring—as he said it—"A glimpse of the light of God's countenance to the comforts of a warm bed."

If such self-discipline, however, be absolutely required for admission to the kingdom, many who are called will be too sleepy to know they have been chosen. There are, after all, night owls as well as early birds. There really are such creatures as authentic night people. They have no objections whatsoever to mornings, except that they come so early, and, try as they may, at any hour before 9:00 A.M. their get up and go has got up and gone back to sleep! A rising time of 7:00 A.M. makes them feel like a person who has been electrocuted and lived.

Night people in the morning are interesting studies in

slow motion. Those of us who are married to such persons have witnessed a variety of physiological phenomena that have fascinated scientists and horse breeders alike: people and horses can, in fact, sleep while standing up.

People can even talk while sleeping, although not very well. For example, a phrase such as "Howuldchalikeyureggs?" while able to be understood by the trained listener, usually means that cold cereal is on the way. Decisions as to whether knives, forks, and spoons are to be placed on the table become major ones, and night people continually risk electric shock as they rest their heads on the toaster, waiting for the bread they forgot to insert in the slots to pop up.

While morning people are always cheerful and buoyant at 7:00 A.M., nothing is more unwelcome to a night person at that hour than good cheer and a pleasant disposition. Indeed, the primary existential question for night persons is to choose between suicide for himself or murder for his spouse and children. Fortunately, night people lack energy to do either, a fact which has undoubtedly added greatly to our country's problem of population control.

Perhaps this indicates that the premise which says early rising is a sign of godliness is a false one. For one thing, those who feel that suffering—even martyrdom—is *prima facie* evidence of moral purity will discover that night people regard early rising as just that: suffering, verily, the twentieth-century equivalent of self-flagellation. Certainly, too, not all the biblical evidence favors early birds. Isaiah spoke of those who "Rise up early in the morning

126

that they may follow strong drink" (Isa. 5:11). The prophet Micah said: "Shame on those who lie abed planning evil and wicked deeds and rise at daybreak to do them" (Mic. 2:1).

Science tells us, furthermore, that within each of us is a psychological clock which provides differing abilities to wake at early hours. Late risers, in short, are not necessarily spiritually decadent. What may have been interpreted as being shifty-eyed is merely the physical inability to focus on any moving object for longer than one minute at a time.

Thus, it may be that even our body-clocks are reminding us that we are saved by grace and not by works. Dragging our bodies out of bed in order to get a head start on earning compliments from God is to miss the point of the gospel. Grouchiness in the morning is no worse than grouchiness at night, and sleepyheadedness is as interesting to watch at 11:00 P.M. as at 7:00 A.M. Perhaps we could all be helped by recalling Jesus' reminder that *all* the birds of the air (night owls *and* early birds) are loved by God. If we take this seriously, we can rest easy and look for ways to serve him night *and* day.

O God of the morning and the night, we thank you for understanding spouses, automatic coffeepots, and instant oatmeal. Watch over night people in the morning, that as they shuffle about and bump into the furniture, they will not do harm to themselves or their families. In the name of him who slept through a storm. AMEN.

29

On turning forty

Turning forty for many men is a traumatic experience. While most jokes about age refer to women, it is an honest-to-goodness fact that many males enter an uncertain period called "midlife crisis" about this time. Statistical records indicate that it is a period of high risk for divorce, extramarital affairs, career dislocations, accidents, and even suicide attempts.

While the crisis is primarily psychological and not due to hormonal changes, it often is precipitated by a man's awareness of his physical deterioration. At forty, many men conclude that if they had known they were going to live this long, they would have taken better care of themselves. When they go to the beach with their families, they notice that young bathing beauties *look away* as they stride by, holding their breath and pulling in their stomachs until they look like contortionists. Their children do not add to their peace of mind, either, when they compare one's left leg and its varicose veins to a roadmap of Louisiana. Nor does anyone need to remind them of their middle-aged and medium-sized paunches which have gradually appeared and hair which is conspicuous by its absence.

At about age forty men discover that their kidneys no longer have the reserve capacity they once did, an awareness that comes during frequent nocturnal visits to the bathroom and the casual but careful locating of restrooms immediately upon entering any public auditorium. Nagged by the knowledge that his sexual capacity is not what it once was, a middle-aged man may grasp at the forms—if not the substance—of youth, occasionally appearing in public in flared slacks, paisley shirts opened three buttons down, and chukka boots. He may try to recapture his youth by eating organic oats for breakfast and prunes for lunch, a diet which is only slightly better than the indigestion it seeks to avoid.

Occasionally, he may even attempt to flirt with young women, an event not unlike a dog chasing a car as it doesn't know what to do when it catches one, either. Other men, more fearful of their children's snickering at them than they are of admitting their age, merely worry anxiously over new life situations. The departure of their children from home may also mean the sudden liberation of their wives. A man of forty, clinging to his regimens for security, will spend a restless night after his wife pokes him awake at 2:00 A.M. to announce: "Dear, I've decided to go to law school and then run for the state legislature. Goodnight, darling!"

Wives and children often demonstrate tender concern and love for middle-aged men, but their solicitations are frequently counterproductive. To warn a ten-year-old child that he shouldn't roughhouse with daddy because his father "isn't as young as he used to be" is about as ego-building as a hemorrhoid examination. A father may also get the impression that some of his better lectures on getting home on time and cleaning up the house have been given before, although his increasing absent-mindedness leaves him unsure. The children, bless their hearts, act attentive, knowing that to err is human and to refrain from laughing is humane.

In this, the graying of America, there are hidden truths waiting to be revealed. The realization that one will probably not live as long as one has lived already forces an individual to recognize the disparity between youth and age, hope and fulfillment. A man learns that he was not born to be young beyond his time. After all, at this writing, Mickey Mouse is forty-seven, Lil' Orphan Annie is fifty-one, and even Charlie Brown has turned twenty-five. The time arrives when a man consciously sacrifices many of his favorite fantasies about sex appeal and success. Raquel Welch will simply have to be denied his charms, and someone else will have to write the great American novel.

So may it be. Those who have passed age forty have discovered benefits about which our youth culture knows little and which are available only to people who have lived through at least three revivals of the wide necktie. The great serendipity is *perspective*—to be able to look forward and backward, to feel confident about some things, and to know that survival to this point is promise for the future.

However many divorces do occur, the couples who are still together are probably going to stay together, and their comfortable familiarity with each other makes the frantic sexual groping of Hugh Hefner's disciples seem pathetic and comical. As surprising as it is to many children who grow up and leave home, their parents may not put on sackcloth and ashes of mourning. They may, in fact, drink a little toast with sugar-free cola in celebration of the return of the car. Some men may even applaud the newly found freedom of their spouses, rejoicing in whatever fulfillment is found and hoping that extra income will not put them in a higher tax bracket.

Thanks be to God, life does *not* begin at forty! With selective memories to sort out unpleasantness and Geritol and Serutan (that's N-A-T-U-R-E-S, spelled backward!) to sustain us, we can look at our lives from their continental divide. If what we see is what is and what was, and not much time is spent in yearning for what might have been, what is yet to come can be anticipated with joy in our hearts and, if necessary, a hot water bottle at our feet.

O God of time, watch over all of us who have passed forty. Grant us wisdom, perspective, and good circulation for the living of the days that remain. In the name of him who belongs to all ages. AMEN.

131

30
On being an example to your children

The principle of isometrics is that you can build muscle by pushing firmly against an unyielding object. Character is built in the same way. Parents who take their roles seriously are intimately familiar with such knowledge, as the cost of character-building includes eternal vigilance, daily dedication, and enough luck to break all the casinos in Las Vegas.

The toughest part is setting an example. It is axiomatic that responsibilty and integrity will not be built if the things we believe in are different from the things we do. Yet, lecturing and preaching to children, especially by fathers, is ever so much easier than setting an example, for a man's best friend is his dogma. Sentences that begin, "When I was your age . . ." are seldom effective as small children can't really believe we were ever their age and, if we were, the dinosaurs are all dead by now.

Simply put, there are no shortcuts. If we want them to tell the truth, we'll have to tell the truth, too, even when we think they aren't listening. If we want them to own up to their mistakes, we'll have to own up to our mistakes. That's why character formation is essentially a religious task. As with religion, you've got to practice it when you don't want to in order to have it when you need it.

Such noble sentiments are severely tested in moments of stress, of which there are legion in most normal, chaotic homes. For example, teaching manners is no easy task, and many a tired adult may long to rest his weary elbows on the table and in the privacy of his home slurp his soup! Yet, there they sit, waiting, the recipients of seventy-times-seven sit-up-straight-and-don't-slouch sermonettes and one hundred nineteen try-to-eat-more-quietly admonitions from their parents. Adult violations are duly noted in a child's dues book or commented upon in a tone of moral indignation last heard when Nathan confronted David.

It is in such moments that a child's character is built and an adult's is refined. Rising above his feelings of fatigue and resisting a natural desire to pull rank, the conscientious parent will admit his evil ways and repent, a reaction which is helped by prayer and the knowledge that throwing hot soup on children is a crime in most states.

Or consider this existential moment. The telephone rings. Since the heavy odds are that the call will be for your teenage daughter, she answers. But wait! The call is for you, and it is from a woman who talks for long hours on short subjects and whose conversation is as edifying as a dripping faucet. The tempter, as they say in church, is near at hand, urging you in a still, small voice to wave your hands frantically while you frame the words with your mouth, "Tell her I'm not home and may never return again." In midmouthing, however, homily number sixteen on "always telling the truth" pops into your mind, and one more opportunity for practicing what we preach presents itself.

These events, of course, are but small pebbles in the avalanche of life, and other falling rocks keep them in perspective. Being stopped by a police officer for speeding when accompanied by four small children and one somewhat larger wife as eyewitnesses clearly belongs in the category of major moral testing. Consider the range of feelings experienced by the driver: (1) *Resentment*—"Why aren't you out catching criminals instead of picking on decent citizens?" (2) *Blaming*—"If Nancy hadn't decided to water the plants, I wouldn't have driven so fast." (3) *Cowardice*—"I wonder if he'll let me off if I tell him I'm dying of cancer?"

Your seven-year-old does not help matters, either, by crying aloud, "Will daddy have to go to jail?" Nor do her mother's words reassure: "No, dear, they'll probably just fine him fifty dollars." All the while it seems as if every passing motorist is smirking and pointing accusative fingers, most of whom are silently bearing witness to that modern moral imperative: "Better him than me."

To admit guilt and accept the consequences with some semblance of dignity in the presence of your family is a major moral achievement. To discuss the matter rationally after the ordeal is over and to explain how police officers help save lives by stopping speeding cars is the right thing to do and no more difficult or painful than

134

having your fingernails pulled out with pliers. Even so, to such deeds are we called.

Fortunately, children are usually very forgiving, which is a difference between them and people. If we are not too extravagantly unfair or dishonest or inconsistent, they'll give us the benefit of the doubt. Therefore, if parents have the good grace to apologize for sins of commission and the good luck not to get caught in their sins of omission, their example may have positive effects on their children.

The presence of children, though, merely reminds us that all men and women are called to live lives of integrity, not just to be examples but because it's the best way to live. In this context children are blessings in disguise, for they not only keep us alert to our moral responsibilities, they almost never say, "I told you so."

O God, thank you for the gift of conscience. Help us to live our lives in such a way that our children will not be ashamed of us and when we die even the funeral director will be sorry. In the name of him whose life was exemplary. AMEN.